simply delicious
vegan

giant green bowls

100 PLANT-BASED RECIPES BY THE CREATOR OF *FROM MY BOWL*

simply delicious
vegan

CAITLIN SHOEMAKER

ABRAMS, NEW YORK

To
anyone who
purchases this book, or
receives it as a gift. May you
always be inspired by, gravitate
toward, and play with plant-based
food. And to tahini, because it's
an underrated ingredient and
I think more people
should like it.

**pumpkin spice
date bites**

contents

introduction

Hey there! I'm Caitlin—blogger, vlogger, photographer, yoga enthusiast, chill acoustic music-lover, and all-around plant obsessive. As in, I eat plants. A lot of them. For the past three years, I've been cooking, writing, styling, photographing, and making videos to share the power of plant-based food with my audiences on Instagram, YouTube, and my blog, *From My Bowl.*

I've made it my mission to prove that unprocessed, whole-plant vegan food doesn't have to be bland, expensive, complicated, or time-consuming—because I know that I feel my best when I eat a plant-based diet.

I was raised as a vegetarian and ate a lot of fruits and veggies growing up, but I also enjoyed more than my fair share of sugary treats, mock meats, and packaged foods with additives and unpronounceable ingredients. Not to mention eggs and dairy, my favorite foods at the time.

Once I realized that the things I put in my body were directly affecting how I looked and felt, I decided to take a closer look at what I was eating. I've always struggled with skin problems, and to be honest, I just didn't feel like my best self. I was interested in plant-based food (thanks to all the beautiful vegan Instagram accounts I followed), but saw veganism as more of a "diet" than a long-term lifestyle. Carrots and hummus are great and all, but how could I possibly give up my ooey-gooey cheese pizza, eggs over easy, and late-night ice cream? (Spoiler alert: You don't have to.) After watching a few documentaries (like *Forks Over Knives* and *Earthlings*) and learning that the factory farm systems producing dairy and eggs were just as harmful as the meat industry, I realized that a vegan diet could be beneficial not only to *my* health, but to the health of the planet and all of my furry animal friends. I wanted to go vegan immediately, but I was nervous! I told myself I only had to try it for a week. After seeing how easy it was on the first *day,* I knew it would be my long-term lifestyle.

Since then, I've been committed to food that is:

- **Whole plant–based:** Every single bite is full of amazing, straight-from-the-ground nutrition. That includes fruits, vegetables, grains, legumes, seeds, and nuts in their least processed state. Just the way nature intended!

- **Gluten-free:** This isn't a requirement for vegans, but I personally feel better when I limit the amount of gluten in my diet. I'm still a sucker for a chewy piece of sourdough or fluffy plant-based pizza crust, but that's more of a special-occasion thing.

- **Refined sugar–free:** It's no secret that refined sugar is no good for your health and can contribute to both minor issues (skin outbreaks, weight gain, lack of energy) as well as chronic conditions like diabetes, heart disease, and even cancer. Instead, my recipes use unrefined sweeteners like dates, coconut sugar, and maple syrup—these are pretty easy swaps, and go down just as sweet.

- **Oil-free:** One of the most interesting things I read about when I was researching a vegan diet is that oils are technically a refined food, and that a lot of a plant's nutrition is lost during processing. As a result, I developed some simple hacks to transition to completely oil-free cooking.

I felt a *major shift* after switching to this way of eating. I was energized, so comfortable in my skin, and so *liberated* from those restrictive eating habits and poor body image I'd developed in my teens. There was just one problem: It was *really* hard to find recipes that fit the requirements above but also tasted . . . *not* like rabbit food? I love my health, but I also love tasty food—who doesn't? So off I went to the kitchen, determined to make plants taste just as delicious as my comforting childhood favorites. That's pretty much how *From My Bowl* was born.

I've been cooking up a storm ever since, and this book is a natural progression of my plant-based mission. I've posted thousands of Instagram photos, uploaded hundreds of YouTube videos, and shared plenty of recipes with my audience on the internet. So I think it's about time that I (politely) sneak my way into your physical kitchen with this book, and show you just how easy, fun, and satisfying plants can be!

I totally get how overwhelming healthy eating can seem—between the adaptogenic lattes and twenty-ingredient morning smoothies, it can sometimes feel impossible to make, eat, afford, and enjoy food at all! But trust me: I'm not about that life. You can make yummy, nourishing food with no more than a few simple ingredients, a pot or two, and twenty to thirty minutes, whether you're throwing together a super-quick meal like Coconut Mango Muesli (page 31) or Chimichurri Quinoa Salad (page 91), or taking it up a notch for brunch or dinner with Zucchini Bread Pancakes (page 41) or Spaghetti Squash Lasagna Boats (page 184).

Just like my personal diet, all of the recipes in this book:

- are **free of the ingredients** that don't make me feel my best (animal products, sugar, gluten, and oil);

- work for a **tight budget** and a **busy schedule**; and

- go really, really **big on flavor**, borrowing characteristics of some of my favorite comforting dishes—but still celebrate plants.

And that, my friends, is what *Simply Delicious Vegan* is all about. So let's head into the kitchen, get cooking, and most importantly, have fun!

my whole-food vegan pantry staples

If a cookbook doesn't come with a pantry staples list, is it really a cookbook? Here's the deal: I'm going to keep this relatively short and sweet. But a little savory, too, of course. Below are some of the ingredients I always keep stocked in my pantry and spice cabinet. All of them come up in this book to some degree, but that doesn't mean you have to have *everything* on hand, all the time. Do what works for you, and always shop within your budget—I'll talk a little more about that later!

GRAINS AND LEGUMES

Quinoa
Brown rice (short-grain and regular)
White rice
Gluten-free pasta
Dried beans (any variety)
Dried brown lentils
Canned white beans and chickpeas (for emergencies!)

BAKING SUPPLIES

Brown rice flour
Chickpea flour
Almond flour
Oats (quick-cooking and rolled)
Arrowroot powder

SWEETENERS

Maple syrup
Coconut sugar
Medjool dates

SPICES AND MORE

Smoked paprika
Garlic powder
Onion powder
Cumin
Cayenne pepper
Nutritional yeast
Black peppercorns
Pink Himalayan salt
Vanilla extract

IN THE FRIDGE/FREEZER

Low-sodium tamari (organic when possible)
Vegetable bouillon (for veggie broth)
Nondairy milk
Leafy greens
Seasonal produce
Gluten-free sourdough bread
Frozen berries

ON THE COUNTER

Garlic
Yellow and red onions
Sweet and regular potatoes
Seasonal fruit
Bananas

FRESH HERBS (GROW YOUR OWN!)

Rosemary
Thyme
Basil

NUTS, SEEDS, ETC*

Almond butter
Peanut butter
Tahini
Raw cashews
Pumpkin seeds
Ground flaxseed
Hemp hearts
Assorted nuts (unsalted, raw, and organic, when possible)

*If you have the fridge space, I highly recommend storing your nuts and seeds in the fridge. It extends their shelf life considerably and prevents them from going rancid—plus it makes them crunchier!

lemon poppy seed granola

tried-and-true gadgets and gizmos

A well-stocked pantry is of practically no use if you don't have the proper tools. Well, unless you want to eat literal whole fruits and vegetables… Here are my top kitchen tools, all of which you will need for this cookbook. But if I could recommend only five tools to you, they'd be a good chef's knife, a large cutting board, an adjustable mandoline, a set of nonstick pots and pans, and some reusable silicone baking mats. I use each of these every day, and can't imagine my kitchen without them.

FOR PREPPING

Large wood cutting board
Chef's knife (you only need one good one!)
Knife sharpener
Mandoline
Vegetable peeler
Measuring cups and spoons
Food scale

FOR COOKING

Nonstick pots and pans
Pot with a steamer basket
Large fine-mesh strainer
Wooden cooking utensils
Big and small spatulas
Whisk

FOR BAKING

Baking sheet
Reusable silicone mats
Unbleached parchment paper
Cooling rack
Loaf pan

APPLIANCES

Good-quality high-speed blender, preferably with a tamper
Air fryer
Instant Pot or other electric pressure cooker

FOR FUNSIES

Silicone muffin tin
Silicone popsicle molds
Silicone donut pan

what the heck is that?

If you're new to the world of plant-based, gluten-free, or refined sugar-free eating, first of all . . . welcome! Second of all, *please* don't panic. There are probably going to be some ingredients in here that you've never heard of before, but the good news is that you can get most of them in your grocery store—you've probably just never looked for them before! Following are a few of my favorites.

Nutritional yeast: Informally called "nooch," this fortified yeast has an umami-rich, cheesy flavor that pretty much all vegans know and love as a cheese substitute. No, it's not baker's yeast, and yes, you can eat it straight out of the package. It's an acquired taste, but once you try it, you may or may not refer to it as "gold crack" afterward. You can also toast it to bring out even more umami flavor (see page 219).

Tahini: Most blended nuts and seeds just have the word *butter* added to them (almond, cashew, peanut, sunflower), but ground sesame seeds are known as tahini. What's the deal with that? Anyway, this nutty (nut-free!) spread has a unique earthiness to it that brings some much-needed depth of flavor to certain recipes. Some tahini can be bitter, thick, and gross—if you've tried one of those, I'm truly sorry. Generally speaking, the less English on the bottle, the better. In terms of US brands, Soom Foods makes an incredibly silky and smooth-tasting tahini. It's the only one I use, and for good reason.

Low-sodium tamari: Tamari is a great gluten-free alternative to soy sauce. Both are forms of fermented soybeans, but soy sauce also includes wheat. Tamari has a darker color and richer flavor. Even if you're not gluten-sensitive I recommend ditching the soy sauce; it simply doesn't taste as great. There are lots of brands of tamari on the market—I'm not too particular, but I do recommend getting a low-sodium organic variety. The regular stuff is just too salty for me—and if you feel a dish isn't salty enough, you can always add a pinch of your favorite salt to help balance things out.

Coconut sugar: Coconut sugar is made from coconut palm sap. Yes, it's still a sugar, and large amounts of it probably aren't good for you—duh! However, unlike regular sugar, it retains a lot of vitamins and minerals during processing, like iron, calcium, zinc, and potassium. It also has a great, caramel-y taste that (again) adds depth of flavor. Notice a theme here?

Ground flaxseed: A lot of people add ground flax to their oatmeal or smoothies, and for good reason—it's a great source of fiber and omega-3 fatty acids. But did you know that it can also work as an egg substitute? All you have to do is mix 1 tablespoon ground flaxseed with 2½ tablespoons water, then set the mixture aside to thicken for 5 to 10 minutes. The only downside to flax is that it goes rancid quickly, sometimes even before you buy it from the store. To avoid this, purchase cold-milled seeds, and *always* store it in the fridge. You can also purchase whole seeds and grind them yourself, but this takes more time.

Oat flour: Do you have quick-cooking oats in your pantry? Cool, you also have oat flour. All you have to do is put those oats in a blender and process on high for 45 to 60 seconds, until a light, fluffy "flour" forms. I like to use oat flour in my recipes whenever possible—it's definitely the most affordable and cost-effective gluten-free flour on the market. Note: If you have a sensitivity to wheat, make sure you're purchasing oats that are certified gluten-free.

Vegetable bouillon: I'm a huge fan of this concentrated vegetable broth paste for several reasons. First, it's cost-effective: One small jar retails for $6 to $8 and makes over 38 cups (9 L) of broth! Second, it's easier to reduce the sodium in your broth; if you're looking to make low-sodium broth, just use ½ teaspoon per 1 cup (240 ml) water instead of the standard 1 teaspoon. And finally, it's low-waste: You only have to make what you need, and can repurpose or recycle the glass jar after you use it up.

Pink Himalayan salt: This mineral-rich salt is not necessary, but I do prefer to use it. Different varieties of salt contain different levels of sodium, so it's not always a 1:1 substitution. I wouldn't recommend using table salt, but you can use a finely ground sea salt instead.

switching things up

For every post on my recipe blog, there is at least one comment asking if someone can swap this for that. I totally get it; you want to use up what you have in your pantry, you have an allergy, or you just don't like a certain food. All of the recipes in this book were created with substitutions in mind, so if it's not listed on this page or in the specific recipe notes, I haven't tried it and don't know if it'll work.

Ground flaxseed can be replaced with *ground* chia seeds, but not whole.

Nut butters are pretty versatile and interchangeable; just keep in mind that whatever one you pick will affect the flavor of the dish. If you have a nut allergy, you can swap out any nut butter with sunflower butter, tahini, or coconut butter. Also, if any recipe in this book has a nut-free substitution, it's listed in the recipe notes. I gotchu, friends with allergies!

Nondairy milk is just what you think it is: *any* form of unsweetened plant-based milk that your heart desires! The main point of nondairy milk is to add a touch of moisture and/ or creaminess to a recipe. Most store-bought milks have about the same macronutrient levels and consistency, so if you can find it, you can use it. I'll usually use almond or cashew milk when recipe testing, but soy, oat, coconut, or rice milk will also work.

Tamari can be replaced with liquid aminos or soy sauce, but the latter is not gluten-free. Coconut aminos are a . . . *decent* soy-free substitute. It's not exactly the same, and I find it to be a lot sweeter than the soy-containing versions. However, if you have an allergy it'll do just fine.

Flours are the most common substitution request I receive, but unfortunately, the trickiest to swap. Each flour has a unique flavor, texture, and level of absorbency; because of this, you *cannot* swap flours one-for-one. If a recipe calls for a specific flour, please use that flour. There's a reason it's there! And just because some people think coconut flour is an exception to the rule, I'll explicitly state it here: Unless the recipe calls for it, coconut flour is *not* a good substitute. Ever.

Arrowroot powder is a starch used for thickening; you can substitute either tapioca flour or non-gmo, gluten-free cornstarch (unless otherwise noted).

how to cook without oil

Oil is a pretty standard ingredient in most cookbooks, but not in this one! Simply put, it's not a *whole food*. Take extra-virgin olive oil, for example. Yes, it does contain healthy fats, but so do olives. And when you eat an olive, you're getting those fats along with fiber, vitamins, and minerals that haven't been stripped due to the refining process. Same goes for avocado oil, coconut oil, and so on.

Does that mean you can never, ever, eat oil again? Of course not! This book, however, aims to celebrate the fact that whole-plant foods can be just as delicious and satisfying as other foods. I personally feel much lighter and more energized when I limit the oil in my diet, especially the oil in processed and fried foods.

The reason oil tastes so good is because it's pure fat, of course, and our bodies need fat to survive. This is *not* a low-fat book, friends. Over the years I have perfected the art of making yummy meals with whole-plant fats (like nuts, seeds, and avocados) without the need for any extra oil. All of the recipes in this book are oil-free, but if you want to transfer some of this knowledge to your other favorite recipes, here are some little hacks. After you get the hang of them, you'll see how easy it is to ditch that glass bottle (and your grocery bill will thank you, too!).

cooking

HARDWARE ESSENTIALS: NONSTICK POTS AND PANS

- **To sauté vegetables,** use 2 to 4 tablespoons water or vegetable broth in place of oil, adding more to the pan in 2-tablespoon increments if your pan gets dry. Vegetable broth will give the food more flavor, so I try to use that whenever I have some on hand. You can also sauté your dishes in olive brine if you're looking for some salty, buttery flavor!

- **To caramelize onions or peppers,** add the veggies to your pan with a splash of broth or water, then bring the heat to high and allow all the liquid to evaporate from the pan. Let the veggies cook in the dry pan for 2 to 3 minutes— you may notice some brown or black bits forming around their edges. Add a small splash of water and use a wooden spoon to scrape up all that goodness from the bottom of the pan. (That's called "deglazing" in fancy-chef-speak.) Repeat this process until tender; more deglazing = more flavor!

- **For rice and pasta,** rinse your rice thoroughly with water *before* cooking to reduce its starchy content (which can make it stickier). Rinse your pasta *after* cooking to prevent sticking, if you are serving it plain.

If you plan to use a sauce, don't rinse it; toss the noodles with a little of the sauce before storing your leftovers in the fridge to keep everything nice and lubricated.

roasting

HARDWARE ESSENTIALS: SILICONE BAKING MATS

- **When roasting vegetables,** use a reusable silicone mat to prevent the vegetables from sticking to the roasting pan or baking sheet.

- **Add spices:** If your vegetables are "moist" (think squash, bell peppers, and zucchini), just sprinkle your choice of seasoning over the veggies and give them a toss until evenly coated. If your vegetables are "dry" (mushrooms, broccoli, asparagus), toss with 1 to 3 teaspoons water, tamari, or nut milk to help the spices stick.

- **Use the broiler:** When your veggies are nice and tender, stick them under the broiler on high—with the oven door ajar—to crisp them up. This will only take a minute, so keep a close eye on them!

baking

HARDWARE ESSENTIALS: SILICONE MOLDS AND PARCHMENT PAPER

- **You won't need a cooking spray substitute** if you use silicone baking molds or line your baking tins with parchment paper.

- **For casseroles or similar dishes,** add a thin layer of sauce or vegetable broth to the bottom of the pan before adding any additional ingredients. The broth will evaporate as everything cooks.

- **Great oil substitutes in baking recipes** include nondairy milk, unsweetened applesauce, and nut or seed butters. This does depend on the recipe, though, and will take a little practice to perfect.

1 | waking up

Breakfast: Some of us love it, some of us find it easier to just skip it. Wherever you fall on that spectrum, there's a recipe here for you! This chapter is full of nourishing, satisfying, and easy-to-make recipes that will get food on your plate and get you out the door in no time. All of these recipes can be prepped ahead of time and require minimal day-of assembly, making your morning flow (or stumble) that much easier.

broccoli cheddar
"egg" cups

lemon poppy seed granola

Granola is definitely my favorite homemade snack. It's easy to prepare, makes your house smell amazing, and stays fresh for weeks! It's also a perfect way to use up pantry odds and ends; as long as the wet-to-dry ingredient ratios stay the same, you're pretty much in the clear. These crunchy clusters of lemon poppy seed granola are perfect as toppings for smoothies or nondairy yogurt, or simply for eating by the handful. While some granolas can be overly sweet (and in my opinion, heavy) this recipe brings a zippy kick of lemon to keep things light and refreshing. Don't forget to bake the granola on the bottom rack of your oven for ultimate crispiness! It will also firm up as it cools, so don't be afraid if it looks a little soft when coming out of the oven.

⅓ cup (110 g) grade A maple syrup

⅓ cup (90 g) cashew butter

Juice and grated zest of 1 small lemon (1 to 2 tablespoons)

1 teaspoon vanilla extract

½ teaspoon pink Himalayan salt

3 cups (315 g) rolled oats

¾ cup (105 g) raw cashew pieces

¾ cup (35 g) unsweetened coconut flakes

2 tablespoons poppy seeds

1. Preheat the oven to 325°F (165°C) and line a baking sheet with a silicone mat or parchment paper.

2. Whisk the maple syrup, cashew butter, lemon juice, lemon zest, vanilla, and salt together in a large bowl. Add the oats, cashews, coconut, and poppy seeds, then stir until everything is evenly coated.

3. Use a spatula to spread the granola mixture evenly onto the prepared baking sheet. Bake on the bottom rack of the oven for 20 minutes. Remove from the oven and use a spatula to flip the granola; it will break apart, but just try to make sure most pieces get turned over. Return to the oven and bake for an additional 10 minutes, then remove and let cool completely.

4. Serve as desired; store leftovers in an airtight container at room temperature for up to 1 month. If you have the space, though, I'd recommend storing it in the fridge—it makes everything even crunchier!

note: To make this recipe nut-free, replace the cashew butter with tahini, and the cashew pieces with pumpkin seeds or extra coconut.

morning glory muffins

The ultimate on-the-go breakfast, these one-bowl muffins are packed with wholesome ingredients like carrots, apples, and walnuts. Sort of like a muffin-meets–granola bar, these subtly sweetened treats have a chewy, hearty texture that's incredibly satiating; the muffin tops will get nice and crispy, while the insides stay moist. The pumpkin puree acts as a replacement for both eggs and oil—plus it adds extra depth of flavor! I love to toast one or two of these muffins and enjoy with a dollop of almond butter and a hot cup of coffee. If you have a nut allergy you can easily replace the walnuts with pumpkin seeds or sunflower seeds.

2½ cups (285 g) quick-cooking oats, blended to make oat flour

⅔ cup (110 g) coconut sugar

1 tablespoon ground cinnamon

1 tablespoon baking powder

½ teaspoon pink Himalayan salt

1 (15-ounce/425 g) can pumpkin puree

Juice and grated zest of 1 orange (about ¼ cup/60 ml)

1 teaspoon vanilla extract

1 Granny Smith apple, finely diced

2 cups (195 g) shredded peeled carrots

½ cup (80 g) raisins

½ cup (25 g) unsweetened coconut chips

½ cup (55 g) walnuts, coarsely chopped

1. Preheat the oven to 350°F (175°C) and line a 12-cup muffin tin with parchment paper or liners.

2. Whisk the oat flour, coconut sugar, cinnamon, baking powder, and salt together in a large bowl. Add the pumpkin puree, orange juice, orange zest, and vanilla; use a spatula to mix until a thick, even batter forms.

3. Fold the apple, carrots, raisins, coconut, and walnuts into the batter until evenly incorporated, then evenly divide the batter among the cups in the muffin tin. The cups will be completely full and the batter will be rounded on top (they won't rise much in the oven).

4. Bake for 25 minutes, then carefully transfer the muffins to a wire rack and let cool completely. Serve as desired; leftovers will keep at room temperature for up to 5 days, or can be frozen and reheated as desired; they'll last in the freezer for up to 1 month.

note: Use a food processor with a grater attachment to prepare the carrots, if you have one. It will cut the hands-on time in half!

Hands-on time:	Cook time:	Makes 2 or 3 small toasts;
5 MINUTES	**5 MINUTES**	serves 2 or 3

"everything" avocado toast

Like most millennials, I've made avocado toast a steady staple in my diet. It's my perfect busy-day lunch because all you really have to do is toast some bread, mash some avocado, and sprinkle some chunky salt on top!

While a simple avo mash often does the trick, I also like to get a little creative with my toast, because, well, I'm a total foodie at heart. And this ten-minute toast? It's pretty much . . . everything. First we'll spread a healthy layer of some garlicky Kale Pesto over our toasty bread. Then we'll top it with chunks of avocado for some textural variation, and finally we'll sprinkle some homemade everything bagel spice on top for extra crunch and flavor. Is there really anything else you can ask for?

2 or 3   pieces gluten-free sourdough
bread

3   tablespoons Kale Pesto
(page 219)

½   large avocado, diced

1   teaspoon Everything Bagel
Spice Blend (recipe follows)

Coarse sea or salt or Maldon salt

1. Toast the bread to your desired level of doneness.

2. Spread the pesto evenly over the toast, then top with the avocado, spice blend, and a sprinkle of salt. Serve immediately.

note: Vegan and gluten-free bread can be tricky to find sometimes. If you don't have a gluten sensitivity you can use a gluten-full variety, or you can also roast some sweet potato wedges for a totally grain-free twist!

everything bagel spice blend

Makes ⅓ cup

2   tablespoons dried minced
onion

1½   tablespoons poppy seeds

1   tablespoon sesame seeds

½   teaspoon garlic powder

½   teaspoon pink Himalayan salt
(optional)

Combine the onion, poppy seeds, sesame seeds, garlic powder, and salt (if using) in a small bowl. Mix until well combined, then transfer to a small airtight container and store in a cool, dry place for up to 6 months.

pb&j smoothie cubes

True life: I ate a peanut butter and jelly sandwich for school lunch every day until I was in the fourth grade. After that I couldn't stand the sight of them for years! I still don't enjoy that classic sandwich very much, but I do enjoy the combination of peanut butter, fruity jam, and hearty grains. Quick-cooking oats give this blend a creamy, bread-like flavor that reminds me of both breakfast and a sandwich. Plus, oats are a great source of fiber and complex carbs, meaning you won't get a sugar crash thirty minutes after you drink this.

I prefer to pre-blend all of my smoothie ingredients ahead of time and freeze them in ice cube molds—that way you're not opening a million and two bags and jars when you're trying to make a quick breakfast in the morning. You can use fresh or frozen berries for this recipe, but I prefer to use frozen, as they are often more cost-effective. If you don't have time to let them thaw, you can also microwave them for one minute before adding to the blender. I'd recommend using silicone ice cube molds for this recipe: It makes it a lot easier to pop the cubes out after they harden.

FOR THE SMOOTHIE CUBES:

- ¼ cup (30 g) quick-cooking oats
- ¼ cup (65 g) natural peanut butter
- 2 tablespoons ground flaxseed
- 2 cups berries, thawed for 30 minutes if frozen
- ¼ teaspoon ground cinnamon

FOR EACH SMOOTHIE:

- ½ batch smoothie cubes (above)
- 1 to 1½ cups nondairy milk
- 1 banana or 1 scoop plant-based protein powder

1. Make the smoothie cubes: Put the oats, peanut butter, flaxseed, berries, and cinnamon in a blender. Process on medium-high speed and blend until a uniform, thick paste forms. If your blender has a tamper, you may need to use it to help everything blend together well. If not, pause the blender and scrape down the sides with a spatula.

2. Use a spatula to spread the smoothie base into ice cube molds. Place in the freezer for at least 8 hours, preferably overnight. Use the smoothie cubes as desired, and store any leftovers in the freezer in a resealable bag for up to 2 months.

3. Make the smoothies: Put the smoothie cubes, nondairy milk, and banana in a blender and process until smooth, 45 to 60 seconds. Serve immediately.

notes: This smoothie base isn't too sweet on its own, which is why I recommend blending it with either banana or protein powder to help round things out. I personally love this with my favorite vanilla protein powder, and enjoy it as a post-workout meal all the time!

You can also make the smoothie cubes in a food processor; they may be a little chunky, but will turn completely smooth once blended with milk the next day.

fluffy banana bread

I'm sorry, but does anyone not love a thick slice of banana bread? And how excited would you be if I told you that I've come up with a version that's just as moist and delicious as the original but without the eggs, processed sugar, and flour? This recipe ticks all of those boxes, plus I'd be willing to bet that you have all ten (super-wholesome) ingredients in your pantry right now.

As with all banana breads, make sure your bananas are incredibly brown and spotty. A brown exterior means that more of the starch has been converted into sugar, which makes our fluffy loaf even sweeter. This banana bread does have a long bake time, but that's mostly because vegan baked goods take longer to cook in the oven in general. It's well worth the wait, though. I love to toast my bread slices and enjoy them as-is, but bonus points if you slather them with an extra dollop of nut butter.

---

2 tablespoons ground flaxseed

2½ cups (285 g) rolled oats

2 teaspoons baking powder

1 teaspoon baking soda

½ teaspoon pink Himalayan salt

3 brown and spotty bananas

½ cup (75 g) coconut sugar

¼ cup (135 g) salt-free almond butter

1 teaspoon apple cider vinegar

1 teaspoon vanilla extract

note: You can replace the almond butter with any nut or seed butter, but keep in mind that it will affect the final flavor.

1. Preheat the oven to 350°F (175°C) and line an 8½ by 4½-inch (22 by 11 cm) loaf pan with parchment paper. In a small bowl, combine the flaxseed with 6 tablespoons (90 ml) water. Stir and set aside for 5 minutes, to thicken to an egg-like consistency.

2. In the meantime, put 2 cups (230 g) of the rolled oats in a blender and blend on high speed until a fine flour forms, 45 to 60 seconds. Put the oat flour in a medium bowl with the remaining rolled oats, the baking powder, baking soda, and salt. Mix well and set aside.

3. In a large bowl, mash the bananas with a fork until they have an even, smooth-ish texture. Add the coconut sugar, almond butter, vinegar, vanilla, and flaxseed mixture to the bowl and mix well.

4. Slowly incorporate the dry ingredients into the wet, stirring until all lumps have dissolved. Pour the batter into the prepared pan and smooth the top with a spatula, then bake on the middle rack of the oven for 60 to 70 minutes, until the top is golden brown and a toothpick inserted in the middle comes out cleanly or with minimal crumbs. Let the bread cool for 10 minutes in the pan before transferring it to a cooling rack. Let the bread cool completely before slicing. Leftovers will keep at room temperature for up to 5 days, or can be frozen and reheated as necessary.

broccoli cheddar "egg" cups

These broccoli cheddar cups pack a protein-dense and flavorful punch, thanks to chickpea flour! If you've never worked with this high-fiber, high-protein flour before, don't worry. It's easy to handle and is available in the baking aisle of most grocery stores. I recommend baking these in a silicone muffin pan—you can skip the paper liners, and they'll still pop right out without the need for oil.

2	cups (185 g) chickpea flour (garbanzo bean flour)
½	cup (25 g) nutritional yeast
½	teaspoon ground turmeric
½	teaspoon paprika
1	teaspoon pink Himalayan salt
1	teaspoon baking powder
2	cups (480 ml) nondairy milk
2½	cups (140 g) broccoli florets, cut into bite-sized pieces
¼	yellow onion, finely diced
⅓	cup (35 g) shredded peeled carrots

1. Preheat the oven to 350°F (175°C) and line a 12-cup muffin tin with parchment paper or liners (or use a silicone muffin pan).

2. Whisk the chickpea flour, nutritional yeast, turmeric, paprika, salt, and baking powder together in a large bowl. Pour in the milk and mix until a thick batter forms.

3. Fold the broccoli, onion, and carrots into the batter, then evenly divide the batter among the cups in the muffin tin. Bake for 30 minutes, then remove from the oven and let sit for 10 minutes.

4. Serve immediately, or transfer to a wire rack to cool before storing in the fridge for up to 1 week.

note: Place the silicone muffin pan on a baking sheet before you fill it for easier transfer in and out of the oven.

Hands-on time: 12 MINUTES	**Cook time:** 8 MINUTES	**Makes 8 servings**

coconut mango muesli

Muesli is a Swiss breakfast made from toasted oats mixed with nuts and seeds. This step, while technically optional, makes a big difference in the final product. Oats can be kind of bland on their own, but they take on this wonderfully nutty and sweet flavor after toasting. Believe me: It's worth turning on your oven for, even in the middle of a hot summer's day.

This muesli mix is studded with coconut, macadamia nuts, and chopped mango for a fun tropical twist. We'll also toast both the coconut and macadamia nuts along with the oats to bring out even more roasty flavor goodness! Try to find large pieces of unsweetened coconut, not coconut flakes; the latter will burn too easily in the oven. I also aim to purchase unsulphured, unsweetened mango—sometimes it's a little brown in color, but I'll take that over artificial dyes and sugar infusions any day.

FOR THE MUESLI:

- 2 cups (200 g) rolled oats
- ½ cup (25 g) unsweetened coconut pieces
- ½ cup (70 g) macadamia nuts, chopped in half
- ½ cup (55 g) dried mango, roughly chopped
- ¼ cup (40 g) chia seeds
- ¼ teaspoon pink Himalayan salt

FOR EACH SERVING OF SOAKED MUESLI:

- ½ cup muesli (above)
- ½ cup (120 ml) nondairy milk
- 1 to 2 tablespoons coconut yogurt

OPTIONAL ADD-INS:

- ¼ teaspoon ground cinnamon
- ⅛ teaspoon grated orange zest
- 1 to 3 teaspoons grade A maple syrup or coconut sugar

TO MAKE THE MUESLI:

1. Preheat the oven to 350°F (175°C).

2. Spread the oats, coconut, and macadamia nuts evenly across a baking sheet (no need to line it) and bake on the top rack of the oven for 8 minutes, until the coconut turns golden brown and the mixture is fragrant. Remove from the oven and transfer to a large bowl with the mango, chia seeds, and salt; mix until evenly combined, then transfer to a large sealable jar. Store in a cool, dark place for up to 1 month.

TO MAKE A SERVING:

3. Put the muesli in a small jar or sealable container with the milk, yogurt, and any additional add-ins. Mix well, then place in the fridge to let thicken for at least 3 hours, preferably overnight.

4. Top as desired and serve cold. The soaked muesli can be prepped ahead of time and will keep for up to 5 days in the fridge.

note: If you can't find nondairy yogurt in stores near you, it's not the end of the world. It adds an extra layer of creaminess and tartness to the muesli, but isn't essential to the final product.

zucchini cornmeal "biffins"

Kind of like a biscuit, kind of like a muffin, these zucchini cornmeal "biffins" are a cute-sounding savory baked good that can serve as either a standalone bite or wholesome side. They have a crispy outer edge and a fluffy center with a decent crumb. As with all of my recipes there's no dairy or oil in these babies thanks to zucchini and, more surprisingly, white beans! I love to sneak legumes into my baked goods whenever I can because they add both moisture and fiber.

I like to serve these biscuits with a dollop of Cashew Cream (page 211) and a generous sprinkle of cracked black pepper. If you have any leftovers, they're great alongside Lentil-Quinoa Stew (page 76) or Tex-Mex Black Bean Chili (page 140). These muffins will stick to paper liners, so try to use a silicone muffin pan. Otherwise, you will need to spray the liners with a touch of nonstick cooking spray to avoid this.

2	tablespoons ground flaxseed
1	zucchini, shredded (about ¾ packed cup/285 g)
1	cup (170 g) salt-free cannellini beans, drained and rinsed, or 1 can
3	tablespoons grade A maple syrup
1	cup (160 g) medium-grind cornmeal
1	cup (125 g) brown rice flour
2	teaspoons baking powder
1	tablespoon nutritional yeast
1	teaspoon pink Himalayan salt
¼	teaspoon ground turmeric (optional, for color)

1. Preheat the oven to 325°F (165°C) and set a 12-cup muffin tin aside. Mix the flaxseed with 6 tablespoons (90 ml) water and set aside for 5 minutes to thicken to an egg-like consistency.

2. In the meantime, use cheesecloth, a nut milk bag, or fine towel to squeeze the zucchini over a bowl, saving the liquid. Set the zucchini aside. Put ⅓ cup (80 ml) of the liquid in a high-speed blender with the beans, maple syrup, and ⅓ cup (80 ml) water. Blend on high speed for 20 to 25 seconds, until smooth. Add the flaxseed mixture, cornmeal, flour, baking powder, nutritional yeast, salt, and turmeric (if using) to the blender and blend on low speed until just combined.

3. Add the zucchini to the blender and blend on the lowest setting to mix it into the batter; if your blender does not have a low speed, transfer the batter to a mixing bowl and fold it in by hand. Divide the batter evenly among the muffin cups, then bake on the middle rack of the oven for 45 to 50 minutes, until a toothpick comes out cleanly and the tops are crispy and slightly golden.

4. Immediately transfer the muffins to a wire rack and let cool completely. Serve as desired; leftovers will keep in an airtight container at room temperature for up to 3 days, or can be frozen for up to 2 months.

pumpkin spice latte chia seed pudding

Call me basic, but I love pumpkin spice. So much so that I'll unashamedly enjoy pumpkin spice infused–treats and desserts year round! I'd argue that this chia seed pudding is far from ordinary, though. It's infused with all of the flavors of that classic fall latte, but doesn't have any of the added sugar or artificial flavoring. Plus, chia seeds are full of fiber, plant protein, and omega-3 fatty acids, which are great for heart health. This nourishing breakfast will carry you through your morning with smooth, usable energy—no caffeine jitters, no sugar crash.

You can make this recipe in a large mixing bowl, but I'd highly recommend using a high-speed blender. It's a lot easier to mix the pudding uniformly and break up any lumps.

1   **(13.5-ounce/398 ml) can light coconut milk**

¼   **cup (60 ml) coffee concentrate (see Note)**

¼   **cup (65 g) pumpkin puree**

2   **tablespoons grade A maple syrup**

1   **teaspoon vanilla extract**

½   **teaspoon pumpkin pie spice blend**

¼   **teaspoon pink Himalayan salt**

½   **cup (95 g) chia seeds**

1. Put the coconut milk, coffee concentrate, pumpkin puree, maple syrup, vanilla, pie spice, and salt in a high-speed blender, then blend on high for 10 to 15 seconds.

2. Add the chia seeds to the blender and blend on the lowest setting for 10 seconds. Let the pudding thicken in the blender for 5 minutes, then blend for an additional 10 seconds. Alternatively, blend the mixture on high for 30 to 35 seconds for a completely smooth texture.

3. Transfer the pudding to a container and let sit in the fridge for at least 4 hours, preferably overnight. Leftovers will keep in the fridge for up to 5 days.

notes: If you don't have a pumpkin pie spice blend in your pantry, make your own using 1 teaspoon ground cinnamon, ¼ teaspoon grated nutmeg, ¼ teaspoon ground ginger, and a pinch of ground cloves. You'll have some leftovers, so I guess you'll just have to make this pudding again!

You can easily make your own coffee concentrate at home: Simply prepare your normal cup of coffee (in whatever way you prefer) with half of the normal liquid.

how to have the best morning ever (according to me)

Ever since I graduated from college and started adulting, I've tried to begin my mornings in such a way that (1) I have the most energy possible and (2) I can take advantage of the time of the day when I'm most productive. I've found that, for me, it's a combination of getting my butt out of bed early, starting with some movement, and calling upon my collection of quick, easy breakfast recipes that can get me to my desk ASAP while keeping me satisfied until lunch.

Look, I'll be honest—I don't do all of this every day. Sometimes life just gets in the way, and that's A-okay. But I *do* know that when I follow this routine, I feel really good and accomplished. So maybe give it a try and see what you think! And we can all work on our consistency together . . . except on the weekends. Weekends are definitely for sleeping in.

1. RISE AND SHINE—LITERALLY!

One of my favorite non-kitchen purchases was a low-frequency red light alarm clock. This handy gadget gradually grows brighter as it approaches wake-up time, so when it's time to get up (6 a.m. for me), it's like being gently nudged by the sun—no screaming alarm, thank you very much. Then when the nice, soft glow wakes me up, the first order of business is setting my alarm again for the next day.

2. SNUGGLE UP AND #GOALS

Take a moment to thank your body and show yourself some love—you're alive, after all! This can be as simple as a snuggle with your pillow, furry friend, or significant other, or you can go all gung-ho and bring out the positive affirmations. After I've had my fill of the warm and cozy stuff, I like to reflect on my goals for the day. *What do I* have *to get done? What do I want to accomplish?* I always have a never-ending to-do list and an overflowing inbox, so it's important for me to pick one or two tasks to really focus on.

3. SAY NO TO THE SCREEN

I keep my phone plugged in across the room from my bed and in airplane mode, no exceptions. I don't want to be tempted to check e-mail, social media, or news updates first thing and risk getting sucked in. This is one way to prevent lying around in bed longer than you want to, and another reason to invest in an alarm clock that isn't your phone.

4. HYDRATE, CAFFEINATE

If you know me, you know that I have at least two beverages sitting with me on my desk at all times. Variety is the spice of life, right? I like to start my out-of-bed routine with water, tea, and/or coffee. Sometimes all three. I treat the process of making my warm beverage(s) like a ritual; it allows me to mindfully prepare something I love while waking up my brain and prepping my body to move.

5. TIME TO FLOW

I *always* start my day with some sort of physical activity simply because it feels good, but also because it gets my energy going. Most days that means yoga, which I've been practicing consistently for several years now; it's by far my favorite way to feel strong and focused. Just as I'm a firm believer in mindfully feeding my body, yoga is how I mindfully *move* my body. I usually take an online class or I'll flow on my own for about an hour—just enough time to get nice and sweaty. When I have the time, I take a few extra minutes to meditate in silence, or just sit with my eyes closed and listen to the music. If I'm planning to go to my favorite yoga class in the evening, I'll take a walk outside in the morning instead. Walking is by far the most underrated form of exercise. You can do it anywhere, there's no special equipment required, and you always feel amazing afterward. It's such a great way to get a jump start on the day.

6. BREAKFAST AND WORK

After taking a quick shower and *maybe* making my bed, I head straight to my kitchen and/or office and start to tackle the day. I gotta be honest with you: I'm not the world's biggest breakfast person. But I fully recognize the importance of the day's first meal, especially when it comes to keeping the hangries at bay. I always make sure that anything I make or grab has a healthy balance of plant protein, fat, and complex carbs. Lucky for you, every recipe in my breakfast chapter has you covered!

I also want to make sure that I'm able to get to my desk as quickly as possible, so I never want to spend too much time in the kitchen at this point. My no-fuss breakfast rotation is usually smoothies and smoothie bowls (especially in the summer); pre-prepped overnight oats or chia pudding that I can top with fresh fruit; or super-simple, no-recipe meals—vegan yogurt topped with frozen berries, ground flaxseeds, and homemade granola, or a sweet potato that I roast and top with some nut butter. Then I raise a spoon (or straw) to myself for getting such a great start. Let's do this thing!

2 | brunch
(aka the best meal of the day)

I'm a big fan of breakfast foods, but never all that hungry in the morning. That's why I think that brunch life is the best life: you get to sleep in a bit, then gobble down all of your favorite morning treats whenever you fancy. Brunch, in my opinion, should be a bit heartier than breakfast—it's replacing two meals, after all. The following recipes require a little more time in the kitchen, but the final (totally yummy) products are so dang worth it. So the next time you're craving brunch, skip the restaurant (and the awful wait for a table) and whip up one or two of these treats instead.

salted caramel french
toast casserole

zucchini bread pancakes

While I love banana bread, zucchini bread is actually my favorite. My mom would grow zucchini every year in our little backyard garden, so it always made its way onto our summer breakfast menu. I still crave it on the regular, but don't always feel like waiting an hour for it to bake in the oven. The solution? Zucchini bread pancakes!

Just like the sweet bread, these pancakes are moist and fluffy inside, crisp and golden on the outside. The shredded zucchini melts into the batter as it cooks—it won't feel stringy in the final product, but you will notice that it's there. Coconut flour helps to absorb some of the moisture from the zucchini, but be sure to squeeze as much liquid out of your squash (using a nut milk bag or tea towel) as you can before adding it to the batter. Chopped walnuts also add a nice element of crunch and buttery flavor; if you have a nut allergy, simply leave them out or replace them with sunflower seeds. But most important, don't forget that drizzle of maple syrup on top!

2 cups (200 g) quick-cooking oats, blended to make oat flour

2 tablespoons coconut flour

½ teaspoon baking soda

1½ teaspoons baking powder

½ teaspoon pink Himalayan salt

2 cups (480 ml) nondairy milk

1 tablespoon apple cider vinegar

3 tablespoons grade A maple syrup, plus more for serving

1 teaspoon vanilla extract

1 cup (190 g) finely shredded and squeezed zucchini (about 1 large)

⅓ cup (35 g) walnuts, finely chopped

1. Put the oat flour, coconut flour, baking soda, baking powder, and salt in a large bowl and whisk together. In a separate, smaller bowl, mix the milk, vinegar, maple syrup, and vanilla together until evenly combined.

2. Form a well in the center of the dry ingredients, then pour the wet ingredients into the center of the bowl; mix until no clumps remain and a smooth and thick batter forms. Add the zucchini and walnuts to the batter and gently fold them in.

3. Heat a large nonstick skillet over medium-low heat, then pour ⅓ cup of the batter onto the skillet. Cook for 3 minutes, flip, and cook for an additional 2 to 3 minutes, until both sides are golden brown. Repeat with the remaining batter; if your skillet is large enough, cook multiple pancakes at once to speed up the process!

4. Serve warm, with a drizzle of maple syrup. Leftovers will keep in the fridge for up to 4 days, or can be frozen for up to 2 months.

note: If you have a well-maintained nonstick pan, you won't need to grease it with any oil—that's why we cook these pancakes low and slow! If your pan is a bit older or not nonstick, however, you will need to use some cooking spray to prevent sticking and burning.

herby tofu scramble

I ate scrambled eggs at least twice a week growing up: They were both quick and easy, so they were a go-to school-day breakfast. Long gone are the days of my egg consumption *and* schooling, but I still crave a good scramble. The biggest difference between now and then? I used to use chicken eggs, but now I use tofu!

There are about a million and two recipes for tofu scramble out there on the internet, and honestly I have an issue with most of them. They're either too dry, too mushy, or just not rich enough. My secret? Simmering extra-firm tofu in excess (creamy) liquid to puff it up and get it nice and fluffy, just like a soft scramble. Oh yeah, and *kala namak*. This Indian salt, also known as black salt, has a strong, sulfuric flavor that actually tastes like eggs.

Most grocery stores don't carry *kala namak*; you will have to purchase it online or at an Indian market. A little goes a long way, so purchase a small bag—it will last you a while. It's also important to note that this salt quickly loses it's eggy, sulfuric flavor with heat, so it's best to add it immediately before serving. It's not as salty as regular table salt, so don't shy away from the amount the recipe calls for. Dill and chives make a light and refreshing flavor combination here, but feel free to switch things up with other herbs as you see fit.

---

1 (14-ounce/397 g) block extra-firm tofu

1 tablespoon nutritional yeast

½ teaspoon onion powder

¼ teaspoon garlic powder

¼ teaspoon ground turmeric (optional, for color)

¼ cup (60 ml) Cashew Cream (page 211)

1 tablespoon chopped fresh dill

½ tablespoon chopped fresh chives

¾ teaspoon *kala namak* (black salt)

Pink Himalayan salt and freshly ground black pepper

1. Heat a large nonstick pan over medium heat. Use your hands to break up the block of tofu into medium-size pieces over the pan, then add the nutritional yeast, onion powder, garlic powder, and turmeric. Mix well; when the mixture starts to sizzle, add the cashew cream and ⅔ cup (160 ml) water.

2. Let the mixture simmer for 7 to 9 minutes, stirring occasionally. Use a spatula to further break up any large chunks of tofu, if there are any. When the tofu has thickened, turn off the heat and fold in the dill, chives, and *kala namak*. Season with salt and pepper to taste, then serve warm. Leftovers will keep in the fridge for up to 5 days, but the scramble will lose its "eggy" flavor with reheating.

note: I like to serve this scramble alongside some gluten-free toast, steamed or roasted veggies, and half of an avocado. You know what they say, though: The world is your (vegan) oyster, so go crazy!

blueberry cardamom bakery muffins

Believe it or not, cardamom is my favorite "sweet" spice! I use cinnamon much more frequently, but that's mostly because the flavor profile of cardamom is pretty unique. If you've never heard of this Indian spice before, I highly suggest you add it to your pantry! You can find it both ground and in its whole form, which look like little green pods. Cardamom pods have a lot more flavor to them, but picking them open to get the black seeds out can be both challenging and time-consuming. Because of that, I usually stick with the preground spice.

An ideal morning coffee or afternoon tea companion, these bakery muffins are quite the treat. Spicy, sweet cardamom pairs perfectly with juicy blueberries that burst in your mouth as you bite into them. And let's not forget that crispy coconut sugar–dusted exterior! While this recipe is refined sugar– and grain-free, it's still made from some pretty rich ingredients. One muffin goes a long way!

---

3 cups (295 g) blanched almond flour

6 tablespoons (45 g) tapioca flour or starch

½ teaspoon ground cardamom

¼ teaspoon ground ginger

1 teaspoon baking soda

¼ teaspoon pink Himalayan salt

½ cup (120 ml) unsweetened nondairy milk

¼ cup (65 g) almond butter

½ cup + 6 teaspoons (95 g) coconut sugar

1 tablespoon apple cider vinegar

1 teaspoon vanilla extract

1 cup (150 g) fresh or frozen blueberries

1. Preheat the oven to 350°F (175°C) and line a muffin tin with six paper liners.

2. Put the almond flour, tapioca flour, cardamom, ginger, baking soda, and salt in a large bowl and whisk together until smooth. In a separate, smaller bowl, mix the milk, almond butter, ½ cup (75 g) of the coconut sugar, the vinegar, and vanilla together until evenly combined. Pour the wet mixture into the dry mixture and stir well.

3. Fold the blueberries into the batter, then evenly divide among the muffin cups; there will be rounded batter on top. Sprinkle

1 teaspoon coconut sugar over the top of each muffin, then bake on the middle rack of the oven for 30 minutes. Allow the muffins to cool for 10 minutes before removing them from the pan and placing on a wire rack to cool.

4. Leftovers will keep at room temperature for up to 3 days, or can be frozen for up to 2 months and reheated as necessary.

note: If you're using frozen blueberries, use them straight from the freezer. You can also try this recipe with raspberries or chopped mango for a fun twist!

sweet potato and kale skillet

Sometimes I think sweet potatoes get overlooked when it comes to brunch. I mean, we all love them in soups (page 60), salads (page 80), and as a crispy fry-shaped side with our entrées, so why shouldn't we get to eat them for breakfast, too?

This skillet meal is reminiscent of pan-fried breakfast potatoes, but with a whole-food, fall-inspired twist. First we'll caramelize some peppers and onions in a large pan, then we'll toss in a few warming spices, sweet spuds, and leafy kale, sautéeing everything together until it's perfectly caramelized and fragrant. This recipe does make a large amount of food—when I say a large pan, I mean a large pan. If you don't think yours will work, make this in a soup pot instead. You could serve this skillet with some ketchup for a more classic brunch dish, but I much prefer to drizzle it with my Miso Tahini Gravy.

1 cup (240 ml) vegetable broth

1 sweet onion, quartered and sliced

1 red bell pepper, cut into strips

3 cloves garlic, minced

½ teaspoon ground cumin

½ teaspoon smoked paprika

¼ teaspoon dried thyme

¼ teaspoon cayenne pepper

3 medium-large sweet potatoes, peeled and diced; (about 6 cups/950 g)

½ bunch curly or lacinato kale, stems removed, roughly chopped

Salt and freshly ground black pepper

Miso Tahini Gravy (page 216), for serving

1. Put ¼ cup (60 ml) of the broth in a large sauté pan over medium-high heat. When it's warm, add the onion and bell pepper; let the veggies cook down, until no liquid is left and a golden residue begins to form on the bottom of the pan. Deglaze the pan by pouring in ¼ cup of the broth and stir well. Repeat this process with the remaining broth.

2. Reduce the heat to medium-low and immediately add the garlic, cumin, smoked paprika, thyme, and cayenne pepper. Sauté for 1 to 2 minutes, then add the sweet potatoes. Cover the pan and let the sweet potatoes steam until fork-tender, 12 to 14 minutes. Remove the lid and stir the mixture every 5 to 6 minutes, to ensure nothing sticks to the bottom of the pan. Add a splash of water if the mixture gets too dry and starts to stick.

3. Add the kale and sauté, uncovered, until the kale is tender, 3 to 5 minutes. Add salt and black pepper to taste, if necessary. Transfer to serving plates or bowls, then top with gravy. Serve warm.

note: You can use the prebaked pie crust in any recipe of your choosing, whether in this cookbook or not! If the recipe calls for further baking in the oven, cover the edges of the pie crust with foil to prevent burning.

Hands-on time:	Cook time:	Makes 1 (9-inch/23 cm) pie
30 MINUTES	25 MINUTES	or pizza crust

three-ingredient multipurpose dough

There's rarely a time when there's not a batch of this dough in my fridge. I first created it (by accident!) when testing out a gluten-free piecrust for a blueberry pie, but have used it for practically anything and everything since. Fruity pies? Heck yes. Vegan quiches? You betcha. It can even be used as a crispy pizza crust (page 183).

This dough is super versatile, easy to throw together, and will keep in the fridge for up to one week. The almond flour releases its oil as it bakes, meaning you still get that crispy and flaky piecrust we all know and love—without any added oil, or having to grease your baking pan.

- 2 tablespoons ground flaxseed
- 1¼ cups (125 g) blanched almond flour, plus more if needed
- ⅓ cup (40 g) tapioca flour
- ¾ teaspoon pink Himalayan salt

TO MAKE THE DOUGH:

1. In a small bowl, combine the ground flaxseed with 5 tablespoons water and set aside for 5 to 10 minutes to thicken to an egg-like consistency.

2. In a medium bowl, whisk together the almond flour, tapioca flour, and salt. Add the flax "egg" and mix until a dough forms. You can start out with a

spatula or fork, but you'll want to eventually use your hands to really get in there. The dough should be damp but not sticky. If it is, add more almond flour in 1-tablespoon increments until it isn't.

TO USE AS A PIECRUST:

3. Form the dough into a ball and place it between two sheets of parchment paper. Use a rolling pin to roll out the dough until it's wide enough to cover the base of your pie pan.

4. Peel off the top layer of parchment paper, and gently place your pie pan on top of the dough. Flip the pan and dough

over, and remove the other sheet of parchment paper, which should now be on top. Use your fingers to press the dough evenly into the pie pan. Poke several holes in the dough using a fork.

5. Place the pie pan in the freezer for 20 minutes; meanwhile, preheat the oven to 400°F (205°C).

6. Cover the dough with aluminum foil and pie weights (or dried beans), then bake for 15 minutes. Uncover, then cook for an additional 10 minutes.

Hands-on time:	Cook time:	Makes 1 (9-inch/23 cm) quiche;
20 MINUTES	30 MINUTES	serves 6 to 8

sun-dried tomato and spinach quiche

I'd spend at least two weeks of every summer at my grandma's house off the New England coast, and every year (without fail) my aunt and I would make quiche for a family dinner. I didn't want to miss out on that tradition after adopting a vegan lifestyle, so naturally I created my own plant-based version!

First, we'll use the multipurpose dough to make our buttery, plant-based crust. Then, we'll fill it with a chickpea-flour batter similar to the one we use in Broccoli Cheddar "Egg" Cups (page 28). I love the combination of vegetables in this recipe, but you can also treat the batter as a "base" and add any veggies that you'd like. Try to purchase sun-dried tomatoes that are dried naturally, without oil; they're just as flavorful, and rehydrate well with just a bit of heat and liquid. This quiche can be enjoyed cold, but it reheats well, too! You can also freeze pre-sliced leftovers and defrost as necessary.

---

1 batch Three-Ingredient Multipurpose Dough (page 49), prebaked into a piecrust

1 cup (240 ml) vegetable broth

1 small yellow onion, cut into ½-inch (12 mm) rings and quartered

½ cup (60 g) packed sun-dried tomatoes, roughly chopped

4 ounces fresh baby spinach

1 cup (85 g) chickpea flour (garbanzo bean flour)

¼ cup (20 g) nutritional yeast

½ teaspoon baking powder

½ teaspoon ground turmeric

½ teaspoon pink Himalayan salt

1 cup (240 ml) nondairy milk

1. Preheat the oven to 350°F (175°C) and prebake the piecrust in a 9-inch (23 cm) pie pan, if you haven't already.

2. Put ¼ cup (60 ml) of the broth and the onion in a nonstick pan over medium-high heat. Sauté until all of the liquid has evaporated, then let the onion sizzle in the pan for an additional 15 to 20 seconds. Deglaze the pan by pouring in an additional ¼ cup broth and stirring the onion around with a spatula; repeat with the remaining stock to caramelize the onion.

3. Add the last of the vegetable broth to the pan, along with the sun-dried tomatoes, then reduce the heat to medium-low. Cook for 2 to 3 minutes, then fold in the spinach and cook until just wilted. Remove from the heat and set aside.

4. Whisk the chickpea flour, nutritional yeast, baking powder, turmeric, and salt together in a large bowl. Pour in the milk and mix until no lumps remain. Fold in the cooked veggie mixture, then transfer the batter into the piecrust. Use a spatula to even out the top and smooth out any lumps.

5. Bake for 30 minutes. Let cool for 10 minutes before slicing and serving.

salted caramel french toast casserole

French toast casserole always reminds me of Christmas. I distinctly remember my mom dousing some bread in a sweet, creamy sauce on Christmas Eve, then tucking it away in the fridge for an easy and quick pop-in-the-oven breakfast the next day. While it does make a great fuss-free holiday recipe, I'm now a believer that this yummy brunch treat should be enjoyed year round, especially when it's soaked in an irresistible-but-somehow-pretty-good-for-you salted caramel sauce ;)

This casserole takes less than 5 minutes to put together the night before your brunch, which is a total win in my book. I find that a gluten-free sourdough bread provides an interesting sweet and sour flavor contrast here, but you really can use any kind you'd like. If you do want to add a holiday twist to this recipe, try replacing the cinnamon with a pumpkin pie, apple pie, or gingerbread spice blend.

1½ cups (360 ml) nondairy milk

1 cup (240 ml) Salted Caramel Sauce (page 215)

2 tablespoons ground flaxseed

1 teaspoon vanilla extract

1 teaspoon ground cinnamon

Pinch of pink Himalayan salt

12½ ounces (353 g) gluten-free sourdough, sliced

1. Whisk the milk, caramel sauce, flaxseed, vanilla, cinnamon, and salt together in a medium bowl; let sit for 5 minutes, to allow the mixture to thicken. Pour ¼ cup (60 ml) of the wet mixture into the bottom of a small glass baking dish and use a spatula to spread it around. Layer the bread slices in the dish so they slightly overlap, then pour the remaining wet mixture evenly over the bread. Cover the dish with aluminum foil and refrigerate for at least 6 hours, preferably overnight.

2. Preheat the oven to 350°F (175°C).

3. Bake the covered casserole on the middle rack of the oven for 30 to 35 minutes, depending on how crispy you'd like your bread edges. Top as desired, then serve warm.

note: I like to keep my bread slices whole for a French toast vibe, but you can also break them up for more of a bread pudding texture.

sweet and smoky tempeh

This tempeh is a staple in my house—I make it at least once a week, without fail. I love it in garlicky grits bowls (page 57), plant-based BLTs, breakfast sandwiches, and chopped up in giant salads, but the serving possibilities are pretty much endless.

If you've never cooked with tempeh before, it's essentially fermented soybeans that have been pressed into a firm block; think of it like a probiotic-infused tofu, with a heartier, less spongy texture. Tempeh has a funky, "tangy" taste to it if you eat it raw, but this goes away with steaming. Most recipes call for marinating, steaming, and frying your tempeh separately, but I've come up with a quick and easy cooking hack that does all three at once! Pan-steaming the tempeh in the marinade infuses it with flavor without having to prep anything in advance; then, once all of the liquid in the pan evaporates, we'll give the tempeh a quick sear to get that shiny caramelization we all know and love—but without any oil!

1	cup (240 ml) vegetable broth
1	tablespoon reduced-sodium tamari
½	tablespoon grade A maple syrup
1	teaspoon liquid smoke
½	teaspoon smoked paprika
¼	teaspoon freshly ground black pepper, or to taste
1	(8-ounce/227 g) package of tempeh

note: This tempeh has a smoky "bacon" taste, but is still soft in texture. If you want to crisp it up, pop it in an air fryer at 360°F (180°C) for 10 minutes, or bake it in a 425°F (220°C) oven for 8 to 10 minutes.

1. Whisk the broth, tamari, maple syrup, liquid smoke, smoked paprika, and black pepper together in a small bowl. Remove the tempeh from the package and cut it into ½-inch (12 mm) strips. Place the tempeh strips in the bottom of a large, nonstick pan and pour the marinade over top.

2. Bring the tempeh and marinade to a simmer over high heat, then reduce the heat to medium-high. Use a spatula to flip the tempeh every 3 minutes, to ensure both sides cook evenly. Continue to flip the tempeh until most of the liquid has evaporated and the marinade starts to look "sticky," 7 to 10 minutes.

3. Reduce the heat to medium-low and begin to frequently flip the tempeh to ensure all pieces and sides are equally browning. After all of the liquid has evaporated from the pan, cook the tempeh for 30 to 60 seconds more to fully caramelize each side. Remove from the heat, and serve as desired. Leftovers will keep in the fridge for up to 5 days.

grits bowls with sweet and smoky tempeh bacon

These bowls are perfect for the savory brunch lover. Creamy, garlic-infused grits with Sweet and Smoky Tempeh (page 54) , sautéed veggies, and fresh tomatoes make for a flavor and texture combination that's hearty, satisfying, and damn delicious. You'll savor every bite (see what I did there?), but won't feel like you need to take a four-hour nap after you finish. That, my friend, is the magic of plants!

It may seem like there's a lot of steps to this recipe, but multitasking is your friend here. You'll have plenty of time to cook the smoky tempeh, mushrooms, and kale while the grits are simmering away. If you're not a fan of kale, swap it out for chard, collard greens, or baby spinach.

FOR THE GARLICKY GRITS:

- 2 cups (480 ml) nondairy milk
- ½ teaspoon garlic powder
- 1 cup (170 g) yellow corn grits
- ¾ teaspoon pink Himalayan salt, or to taste

  Freshly ground black pepper

FOR THE TEMPEH AND VEGETABLES:

- ½ tablespoon low-sodium tamari
- 2 cloves garlic, thinly sliced
- 6½ ounces (185 g) cremini mushrooms, sliced
- 1 bunch curly kale, stems removed, roughly chopped
- 1 batch of Sweet and Smoky Tempeh (page 54)
- 7 to 10 cherry tomatoes, sliced

  Hot sauce (optional)

1. Make the garlicky grits: Put the milk, 3 cups (720 ml) water, and the garlic powder in a medium pot. Bring to a boil over high heat.

2. Slowly whisk the grits into the boiling milk mixture, then reduce the heat to medium-low and cook for 5 to 7 minutes, depending on your desired thickness. Stir occasionally to ensure that nothing sticks to the bottom of the pan. When the grits reach your desired thickness, remove them from the heat and season with salt and pepper to taste.

3. While you're making the grits, put the tamari, garlic, and 2 tablespoons water in a separate nonstick pan over medium heat. When the liquid starts to steam, add the mushrooms and cook for 5 minutes, stirring occasionally. Add the kale to the pan, but do not mix. Cover the pan and steam for 2 to 4 minutes, until the kale is tender.

4. Assemble the bowls by placing a large scoop of grits in the bottom of each, then top with the kale and mushrooms, tempeh, and cherry tomatoes. Serve immediately—sometimes I like to add a little drizzle of hot sauce on top for an extra kick!

how to make your food look as pretty as you

Well, hey there gorgeous.

Look, I get it: You've just spent *way* too much time in the kitchen to make a meal for your family and friends. *You* know that it tastes good, but somehow it just looks like a plate of lumpy veggies—or worse, brown mush. Sometimes I'm a proud member of the #brownfoodsclub, but sometimes? Sometimes it's nice to sit down to a plate or bowl that looks as great as it tastes. Considering that we all eat with our eyes before our mouths, it truly does help to make the meal feel more special.

Whether you're looking to impress some guests or simply trying to give your foodie pics an upgrade, here are three things to always consider:

- **Contrast:** The reason your brown food looks so boring is because it's all brown. The solution? Color! The plant world is basically an edible rainbow, and I'm pretty sure you can find at *least* one colorful topping that will both complement the flavors of and bring more interest to your dish. When in doubt, a small pop of green always seems to do the trick (think fresh herbs or green onions). If you're feeling more creative, try to consider the color wheel and choose complementary colors, like oranges with blues, purples with yellows, or reds with greens. I'd need a whole separate book to completely explain color theory, but you can learn a lot through a quick Google search.

- **Layers:** Depth of flavor is *key* to a good recipe, but depth is also something to consider when styling your food. Having all of your goodies on one flat plane will make your dish look uninviting. Again, there's an easy solution. All you need to do is add some height! This can be as simple as sprinkling some crunchies on top of a soup, piling up a salad on a smaller plate, or even placing your finished dish on top of a serving tray or table linen.

- **Texture:** Monotony is *boring*. Nobody likes an overly crunchy salad or a totally soft bowl of food. Paying attention to the textures in your food will maximize its enjoyability. For example, a bowl of massaged kale topped with large chunks of roasted sweet potato, thin slices of crisp cucumber, a drizzle of yummy dressing, and a sprinkle of hemp hearts hits pretty much all the marks of crunchy, soft, chewy, and creamy. Not only does this make for a better visual experience, but it also makes for a much more pleasurable eating experience.

3 | for slurping

Soup is just great. It's filling, perfect for meal prep, and is a fantastic way to use up veggie odds and ends in your fridge. I always have some variety of frozen soup in my freezer for those can't-be-bothered-to-cook days. Whether you're craving something refreshing (Cucumber and Roasted Red Pepper Gazpacho, page 79), ultra-cozy (Tomato Soup 2.0, page 64), or something in between (Lentil-Quinoa Stew, page 76), I firmly believe there's a soup out there for everyone.

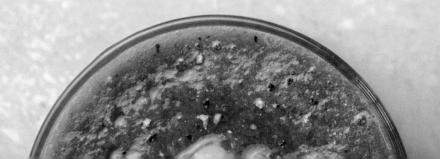

cucumber and roasted
red pepper gazpacho

broccoli cheddar soup

Forget chicken noodle, broccoli cheddar soup was always my personal favorite! This plant-based version is just as satisfying and cheesy, thanks to cashews, gold potatoes, and nutritional yeast. I've yet to come across a gluten-free bread bowl, but you can always top your soup with some Stupid Easy Croutons (page 123) if you're craving an extra-carby bite.

One of my pet peeves with broccoli cheddar soup is super-soft, almost-yellow broccoli. C'mon, where's the fun in that? Using fresh broccoli (not frozen) is a total game changer here—it won't turn to mush, plus you can cook it to your desired tenderness. I like to finely chop mine for that classic soup texture, but you can also save some prep time and leave it in bigger chunks, if that's your thing.

1 large peeled carrot

1 pound (455 g) gold potatoes, cut into small pieces

½ cup (70 g) raw cashews

½ teaspoon garlic powder

½ teaspoon onion powder

½ teaspoon smoked paprika

6 cups (1.4 L) vegetable broth

½ cup (30 g) nutritional yeast

4 cups (205 g) broccoli florets, finely diced

1. Shred ⅓ cup (35 g) of the carrot, then roughly chop the rest. Set the grated carrot aside, and add the chopped portion to a large pot with the potatoes, cashews, garlic powder, onion powder, smoked paprika, and broth. Cover the pot and bring to a boil over high heat; keep covered once boiling, but reduce the heat to medium-high. Cook for 8 minutes, or until the carrots are fork-tender.

2. Reduce the heat to medium-low and use a wide slotted spoon to transfer all of the potatoes, carrots, and cashews to a high-speed blender, along with the nutritional yeast and 1½ cups (360 ml) of the broth. Add the broccoli and shredded carrot to the remaining broth in the pot and let simmer while you blend the potato mixture for 60 seconds, until smooth and creamy. Pour the potato mixture back into the pot, stir well, and let the soup simmer for an additional 1 to 2 minutes. If the soup is too thick, loosen it with warm water to your liking.

3. Ladle into serving bowls and serve warm. Leftovers will keep in the fridge for up to 5 days, or can be frozen for up to 2 months.

tomato soup 2.0

I loved tomato soup as a kid—who didn't? Looking back, though, there was definitely something off about those tangy, almost-too-sweet cans of condensed . . . stuff. Nowadays I don't think I would even touch it with a ten-foot pole, let alone put it in my mouth.

Luckily for all of us, it's still possible to make and enjoy some good-a**, super-satisfying, creamy tomato soup—with only seven ingredients! I call this recipe "Tomato Soup 2.0" because it takes the classic flavor profile to the next level, thanks to fire-roasted tomatoes and some sneaky roasted red peppers. The recipe calls for full-fat coconut milk instead of dairy cream for that full-bodied, thick consistency that glides off of your tongue—but not before dancing with your taste buds.

---

1 shallot, sliced

2 cloves garlic, roughly chopped

2 cups (480 ml) vegetable broth

1 (13.5-ounce/400 ml) can full-fat coconut milk

2 (28-ounce/794 g) cans diced fire-roasted tomatoes

12 ounces (340 g) roasted red peppers, roughly chopped

1 (6-ounce/170 g) can tomato paste

Salt and freshly ground black pepper

Stupid Easy Croutons (page 123)

1. Heat a large nonstick pot over medium heat and add ¼ cup (60 ml) water, the shallot, and garlic. Sauté until the shallot is translucent, 5 to 7 minutes.

2. Stir in the broth, coconut milk, tomatoes, roasted peppers, and tomato paste and increase the heat to high. Bring to a boil, reduce the heat to low, and let the soup simmer for 10 to 15 minutes.

3. Use an immersion blender to blend the soup until it's nice and smooth, or carefully transfer the soup to a blender and do the same. Season with salt and black pepper to taste, if necessary. Top with the croutons, then serve warm. Leftovers will keep in the fridge for up to 5 days, or can be frozen for up to 2 months.

curried carrot soup

Silky-smooth and creamy, this carrot soup has a spicy kick thanks to lots of fresh ginger and warming curry spices. If you can't handle the heat, you can reduce the amount of ginger the recipe calls for by half. Every curry powder blend tastes a little different, so feel free to use your personal favorite. Try to find a salt-free blend, though; otherwise you will need to replace some of the vegetable broth with water.

Canned light coconut milk gives this soup plenty of body and depth of flavor without a whole lot of fat, but you can also use full-fat if you're looking for an uber-rich and creamy bisque. This soup is great for lazy cooks: You don't have to chop any of the vegetables too finely, as it's all getting blended together anyway. If you like a crunchy element to your soup, top this puree off with a handful of pumpkin seeds or some Stupid Easy Croutons (page 123). Sometimes I use leftovers as a nontraditional pasta sauce; it sounds strange, but don't hate it until you try it.

---

1 small yellow onion, diced

1 rib celery, sliced

3 cloves garlic, roughly chopped

1 tablespoon chopped peeled fresh ginger (2-inch/5 cm piece)

2 to 3 teaspoons salt-free curry powder, to taste

1 (13.5-ounce/398 ml) can light coconut milk

3 cups (710 ml) low-sodium vegetable broth

6 carrots, peeled and roughly chopped

Salt and freshly ground black pepper

1. Heat a large nonstick pot over medium heat and add ¼ cup (60 ml) water, the onion, and celery. Sauté for 5 minutes, or until the onion is translucent. Add the garlic, ginger, and curry powder to the pot and sauté for 1 to 2 minutes, stirring well.

2. Set 2 tablespoons of the coconut milk aside to top the bowls of soup later, then add the remainder of the can to the pot, along with the broth and carrots. Raise the heat to high and bring to a boil, then reduce the heat to medium-low and simmer for 10 to 12 minutes.

3. Use an immersion blender to blend the soup completely, or transfer the soup to a high-speed blender and blend on high for 30 to 45 seconds, until completely smooth. Return to the pot and season with salt and pepper to taste. Transfer to serving bowls and top with a drizzle of coconut milk.

peanut butter and sweet potato soup

I know, I know. Peanut butter, sweet potatoes, and tomatoes . . . together . . . in a soup? This is one of those recipes where you're just going to have to trust me. It may sound strange, but this unique flavor combination is rich, creamy, and has deep, deep flavor. I wish I could claim it as my own invention, but it's a pretty classic combination in West African stews. I actually first tried it while attending my first vegan food festival in college—just one bite and I was hooked!

Try to find canned fire-roasted diced tomatoes; they have an amazing flavor profile and provide a nice body to the soup. The natural peanut butter I use contains salt, but if yours is unsalted you may need to add additional salt to taste. Sweet potatoes add a great starchy component to this soup, but I've also made it with butternut squash for a lighter take. Sometimes I also throw in a handful of baby spinach or chopped kale at the end of the cooking process—you know, for the #health.

---

1 small yellow onion, diced

3 cloves garlic, minced

2 teaspoons ground cumin

½ teaspoon cayenne pepper (or less if you're sensitive to heat)

1 (6-ounce/170 g) can tomato paste

½ cup (145 g) natural peanut butter

1 (28-ounce/794 g) can diced fire-roasted tomatoes

5 cups (650 g) cubed peeled sweet potatoes (½-inch/12 mm pieces; about 2 large)

3 cups (720 ml) vegetable broth

Salt

Chopped fresh cilantro

1. Heat a large nonstick pot over medium heat; when it's warm, add the onion and ¼ cup (60 ml) water; sauté until translucent, 3 to 5 minutes. Add the garlic, cumin, and cayenne, then sauté for another minute.

2. Add the tomato paste and peanut butter to the pot and stir it into the vegetables. When it's dissolved, add the diced tomatoes, sweet potatoes, and broth. Bring to a boil over high heat, then reduce the heat to medium-low and simmer for 15 minutes, until the sweet potatoes are fork-tender.

3. Remove from the heat and carefully transfer half of the soup to a blender with a vent; blend until creamy, 45 to 60 seconds. Return the blended soup to the pot and mix well. Add salt to taste, if necessary.

4. Ladle the soup into serving bowls, top with fresh cilantro, and serve warm. Leftovers will keep in the fridge for up to 5 days, or can be frozen for up to 2 months.

note: Peanut allergy? While peanut butter gives the most traditional flavor to this soup, I've found that sunflower butter results in a pretty similar flavor.

green curry soup with zucchini noodles

Is there really such a thing as too much green curry? I sure don't think so, which is why I decided to make that spicy, rich, and sweet sauce last even longer in my bowl . . . by turning it into a soup and adding a ton of veggies! Many Thai restaurants will fry their curry paste in order to bring out more flavor, but I find that sautéing mine in coconut cream gives a similar result.

If you can't find kabocha squash near you, a peeled and chopped sweet potato will do the trick. I prefer to lightly cook my zucchini noodles, but you can also serve them raw for extra crunch, too. You can also top this soup with some crispy tofu (see page 171) for an extra boost of protein.

1   (13.5-ounce/400 ml) can full-fat coconut milk, refrigerated overnight

4 to 6   (65 to 100 g) tablespoons green curry paste (see Note)

2   tablespoons tamari

1   teaspoon coconut sugar

2   cups (275 g) cubed kabocha squash

1   red bell pepper, sliced into strips

1   (8 ounce/227 g) can bamboo shoots, drained and rinsed

1   zucchini, spiralized into "noodles"

1   cup (100 g) bean sprouts

Fresh Thai basil

1. Heat a large pot over medium-high heat. Open the can of coconut milk and use a spoon to scoop ¼ cup (60 ml) of the thicker coconut cream at the top of the can into the pot. When the cream has melted, add the curry paste and "fry" for 60 to 70 seconds.

2. Add the remaining liquid from the coconut milk can, along with the tamari and coconut sugar; whisk until the sugar dissolves completely. Add the squash, bell pepper, bamboo shoots, and 3 cups (720 ml) water. Bring to a boil, then reduce the heat to low and simmer for 10 to 15 minutes, until the squash is fork-tender. If you would like to lightly cook your zucchini noodles, add them to the soup for the last 2 minutes of cooking.

3. Divide the soup among four bowls, then top each bowl with bean sprouts and basil. Serve warm.

note: If you're looking for a mild curry flavor or are sensitive to heat, add 4 tablespoons curry paste to start—you can always stir more into the soup broth later! If you know you like it spicy, go ahead and add all of it.

butternut bean bisque

Dare I say that this soup is the perfect fall recipe? Butternut squash, hearty white beans, and cashew cream combine with fragrant warming spices to make this cozy and comforting soup. It's best served alongside an oversized sweater, giant fuzzy blanket, and a gray autumn day, but it's just as delicious at the regular ol' dinner table as well. It can comfortably serve four with some crusty bread or a side salad, or two hungry plant eaters as a main course. You can also make a big batch of this and store individual-size portions of soup in your freezer for those days when you can't be bothered to cook.

Not only is this soup nourishing and satisfying, but it's pretty budget friendly, too. Butternut squash is technically in season during the summer and fall, but it keeps practically forever in your pantry—so if you see a good sale at the store, stock up!

---

5 cups (1.2L) low-sodium vegetable broth

1 large shallot, diced (about ⅓ cup, 60 g)

1 rib celery, diced

½ tablespoon finely chopped fresh rosemary

1 teaspoon finely chopped fresh thyme

½ teaspoon smoked paprika

Freshly ground pepper

1 butternut squash, peeled and cubed (about 5 cups, 675 g)

2 cups (320 g) cooked navy beans (or great northern, or cannelini)

½ cup (120 ml) Cashew Cream (page 211)

Salt

1. Heat a large nonstick pot over medium heat and add ¼ cup (60 ml) of the broth. Add the shallot and celery, then sauté until translucent, 3 to 5 minutes. Add the rosemary, thyme, smoked paprika, and black pepper to taste, then sauté for an additional minute.

2. Add the squash to the pot and sauté for 1 minute; if things start to stick, add an extra splash of broth. Add the beans and the remaining broth, then bring to a boil over high heat.

3. When the soup starts to bubble, reduce the heat to medium-low and simmer, uncovered, for 15 minutes, or until the squash is fork-tender. Carefully transfer 4 cups (960 ml) of the soup to a blender and add the cashew cream; blend on high speed for 30 to 40 seconds, until smooth and creamy. (Alternatively, use an immersion blender to blend one-third to one-half of the soup right in the pot.)

4. Return the blended soup to the pot, stir, and season with salt and additional pepper, if necessary. Serve warm; leftovers will keep in the fridge for up to 7 days, or can be frozen for up to 2 months.

creamy corn chowder

Or CCC, for short ;) A chowder is a form of thick soup that's often made with a dairy milk or cream base and thickened with crackers. We're skipping both of those today and thickening our soup with cashew cream and potatoes instead! The starchy component of gold potatoes gives this soup a great body and thickness, while the cashew cream adds that extra oomph of healthy fats (and magnesium!) to make this soup one to remember. If you have a tree nut allergy you can replace it with coconut cream, but this will affect the final flavor of the soup.

There's one more secret to an amazing corn chowder: pan-searing the corn! This helps to bring out the inherent sweetness of the corn before it's simmered until tender. If you have a nonstick pan, you can easily do this without any added oil. Simply sauté the corn for a few minutes, then deglaze the pan with some vegetable broth to get all of those browned flavor bits into the soup.

- 4 cups (565 g) sweet corn kernels (from about 5 ears)
- 4 cups (960 ml) low-sodium vegetable broth
- ½ yellow onion, diced
- 1 rib celery, diced
- ½ teaspoon smoked paprika
- ½ tablespoon finely chopped fresh thyme
- ½ teaspoon freshly ground black pepper, or more to taste
- 1 pound (455 g) gold potatoes, peeled and cut into ½-inch cubes (about 4 medium)
- ½ cup (120 ml) Cashew Cream (page 211)
- Salt
- Chopped fresh chives

1. Heat a large nonstick pot over medium heat; when it's warm, add the corn kernels and cook for 5 to 6 minutes, stirring every 90 seconds. The corn will become translucent and parts of it will brown and stick to the bottom of the pot.

2. Deglaze the pot by pouring in ½ cup (120 ml) of the broth; use a spoon to remove any pieces of corn that have stuck to the bottom of the pan. Add the onion, celery, paprika, thyme, and pepper, then sauté until the onion is translucent, 4 to 5 minutes.

3. Add the gold potatoes to the pot with the remaining broth and 2 cups (480 ml) water. Raise the heat to high; when the mixture starts to simmer, reduce the heat to medium-low. Cook for 15 minutes, until the potatoes are fork-tender.

4. Transfer 2 cups (480 ml) of the soup to a high-speed blender. Add the cashew cream to the blender and blend on high speed for 30 to 40 seconds, with the blender vent open. Pour the smooth liquid back into the pot and stir to combine. Season with salt and pepper to taste, if necessary.

5. Transfer the soup to serving bowls and top with chives. Serve warm; leftovers will keep in the fridge for up to 5 days, or can be frozen for up to 2 months.

lentil-quinoa stew

This soup is packed with flavor, fiber, and plant-based protein—all thanks to some caramelized veggies, lentils, and quinoa! It's made from only ten budget-friendly ingredients, making it a perfect weeknight staple on those chillier days. The lentils and quinoa rehydrate while simmering in the soup broth, which not only infuses them with extra flavor, but also helps thicken the soup into a hearty stew.

This is one of those recipes that's very easy to double (or even triple) and store in your freezer for a later date. Freezing the soup in single-sized portions makes thawing and using them even easier!

4 cups (960 ml) vegetable broth

1 yellow bell pepper, diced

1 green bell pepper, diced

½ large yellow onion, diced

½ teaspoon finely chopped fresh thyme

½ teaspoon freshly ground black pepper

1 (14½-ounce/411 g) can diced fire-roasted tomatoes

1 cup (195 g) uncooked brown lentils

½ cup (80 g) uncooked quinoa

4 ounces (115 g) baby spinach

1. Heat a large nonstick pot over medium-high heat; when it's warm, add ¼ cup (60 ml) of the broth, the bell peppers, and onions. Sauté for 5 to 6 minutes, stirring occasionally.

2. Let the peppers and onions sit in the pot for an additional 60 seconds after all of the liquid evaporates from the pan. Deglaze the pan by pouring in an additional ¼ cup (60 ml) broth, then add the thyme, black pepper, and diced tomatoes.

Sauté for an additional 1 to 2 minutes, then add the lentils, quinoa, the remaining vegetable broth, and 2 cups (480 ml) water.

3. Bring the soup to a boil over high heat, then cover and reduce the heat to medium-low. Simmer for 23 to 25 minutes, until the lentils are tender. Remove from the heat and stir in the spinach until just wilted, then ladle the soup into serving bowls and serve warm.

cucumber and roasted red pepper gazpacho

I'll be honest: I'm totally that person who can eat a piping-hot bowl of soup when it's 90 degrees outside. However, I understand that not all of us believe that soup season is a year-long thing, which is why I created this crisp and refreshing gazpacho!

Gazpacho is a smooth blended soup made of raw vegetables and olive oil—traditionally, that is. I like to switch things up and use roasted red peppers (from a glass jar) in my gazpacho for extra depth of flavor and, surprisingly, creaminess. I'm a textural eater, so I top my gazpacho with some finely diced tomato and cucumber for a little extra bite. However you like your soups, I really hope you try this one out; serve it soon after you blend everything together, as the bright flavors start to disappear after just a couple of hours in the fridge.

---

1 large English cucumber

10 small Roma tomatoes (2.75 pounds / 1.25 kg)

1 clove garlic, peeled

1 cup (200 g) roasted red peppers

¼ cup (6 g) loosely packed fresh basil leaves (about 9 large leaves)

2 tablespoons balsamic vinegar

⅛ teaspoon cayenne pepper

½ teaspoon pink Himalayan salt, or more to taste

Freshly ground black pepper

1. Roughly chop three-quarters of the cucumber and 9 of the tomatoes into large, even pieces. Put them in a high-speed blender, along with the garlic, roasted peppers, basil, vinegar, cayenne, and salt. Blend on high speed for 45 to 60 seconds, until the entire mixture is smooth and creamy. Season with more salt and black pepper to taste.

2. Transfer to serving bowls, or place in the fridge for up to 60 minutes to chill. Finely dice the remaining cucumber and tomato and sprinkle them on top of each bowl of soup and serve.

4 | salads and slaws

Call me a stereotypical vegan, but I am obsessed with salads. My day just doesn't feel complete without a large bowl of leafy greens! That being said, we're not just talking about some lame iceberg lettuce topped with wilted carrots and tomato chunks here. These salads are packed with a variety of textures, flavors, and a balance of macronutrients to keep each bite just as interesting—and satisfying—as the next.

curried chickpea salad

Hands-on time:
10 MINUTES

Serves 4 as a side; 2 as a main

crispy chickpea salad with creamy avocado dressing

Crisp greens, crunchy chickpeas, a buttery avocado dressing, and tangy pickled onion come together in a salad that's just as delicious and texturally varied as it is wholesome. It's a great "any occasion" dish; none of the ingredients or flavors are particularly seasonal, and it covers all of the bases for fiber, plant protein, healthy fats, and colorful veggies. It's one of my go-to recipes for potlucks and parties, as both my plant-based and plant-curious friends enjoy it equally. Plus it's naturally gluten-free and allergen-friendly, meaning almost everyone can enjoy it! (Unless you don't like chickpeas or avocados . . . and if that's the case, we need to talk.)

- ⅔ cup (165 ml) Creamy Avocado Dressing (page 220), plus more to taste
- 4 ounces (115 g) mixed greens
- 1 carrot, peeled and shredded
- ½ English cucumber, quartered and sliced
- ⅓ cup (30 g) Quick-Pickled Red Onions (opposite)
- 1 batch Crispy Seasoned Chickpeas (page 124)
- Freshly ground black pepper

1. Pour the dressing into the base of a large bowl, then add the greens, carrot, cucumber, and pickled onions. Toss the salad until all of the leafy greens are evenly coated in dressing.

2. Portion the salad out onto serving plates, then top with the crispy chickpeas and a crack or two of black pepper. Serve immediately.

quick-pickled red onions

Makes about 3 cups

1 medium-to-large red onion

¾ cup (180 ml) apple cider vinegar or distilled white vinegar

¾ cup (180 ml) filtered water

1 teaspoon kosher, sea, or pink Himalayan salt

2 teaspoons sugar

1 teaspoon black peppercorns (optional, but recommended)

Optional add-ins: 3-5 cloves of garlic, 1 teaspoon mustard seeds, 1 chopped jalapeño, or 1-2 teaspoons fresh herbs

1. Slice your onion into half or quarter-size rings. I prefer to slice mine to be about ¼ inch thick, but that depends on personal preference. Use a mandoline if you'd like your slices to be more uniform and/or thinner.

2. Break up the onion slices and stuff them into a quart-size glass mason jar.

3. Prepare the pickling liquid by adding all of the remaining ingredients (see Notes) to a small pot or pan over high heat. Stir the mixture together to dissolve the salt and sugar. Once the liquid comes to a boil, carefully pour it into the glass mason jar and let it sit on your counter until it cools to room temperature. The onion pieces will gradually soften and shrink with time—if any stick out above the liquid in the beginning, press them down with a fork 5 to 10 minutes later.

4. Seal your jar, then store in the fridge for up to one month. These pickled onions will be the most crispy within the first week, then will gradually soften with time. Serve as desired.

notes: I like to add my hard spices (like black peppercorns or mustard seeds) in with the pickling liquid while it's heating up. Otherwise, add your softer add-ins (like garlic or fresh herbs) to the jar with the raw onion.

You can use any sweetener of your choice here. Cane sugar, coconut sugar, maple syrup, and agave are all great options.

caitlin's favorite kale salad

This is my go-to weeknight side salad; it's made of really simple ingredients, but it hits the spot every. dang. time. I actually first made this recipe back when I was in graduate school—I would get home from class late and absolutely starving. I'd quickly take my rice and beans (or whatever I'd meal-prepped for the week) out of the fridge and would whip up this salad while everything else warmed up. And while I do get sick of eating some foods over and over, this is one combination that I don't think I'll ever tire of—seriously, I still eat it to this day!

If you're about to skip this recipe because you think kale is bitter and/or tough to chew, let me stop you right there and say that this recipe is neither. The secret? Massaging the kale in its dressing! This helps to break down the tough cell walls of this leafy green and really work all of that creamy, rich, and tangy goodness in there. Your hands will get messy, but that's nothing a quick rinse at the kitchen sink can't fix. I could easily polish off this entire recipe in one sitting.

---

1   **large avocado**

Juice of 1 lemon (1 to 2 tablespoons)

½   **cup (65 g) sauerkraut**

1   **large bunch curly or lacinato kale, stems removed, roughly chopped**

Freshly ground black pepper

1. Scoop the flesh of the avocado into a large bowl and mash it with a fork. Add the lemon juice and sauerkraut to the bowl and mix until evenly combined.

2. Toss the kale into the bowl, then use your hands to firmly massage the dressing into the kale for 60 to 90 seconds; don't be afraid to really work it in there! The kale will drastically decrease in volume and take on a darker, almost translucent color.

3. Transfer the salad to serving plates, then top with black pepper to taste. Serve immediately.

note: You can use pretty much any type of sauerkraut for this recipe—all we're looking for is something with a briny tang. I often make my own at home, but have also used store-bought kraut (or even kimchi!) with the same results.

cherry and arugula salad with roasted cherry balsamic vinaigrette

Cherries are one of my all-time favorite fruits; my fingers were perpetually stained by their bright-red juices throughout many a childhood summer. To be honest, I can still polish off a bag of them in a day! But sometimes—just sometimes—I like to be a little more sophisticated and put them in a salad. This cherry and arugula salad is bright and refreshing, with peppery arugula and sweet cherries, crisp, cool cucumber, and a tart vinaigrette. Serve this salad alongside some roasted veggies or an Italian-style dish and you won't be disappointed.

Do yourself a favor and buy a cherry pitter; some grocery stores sell them, and they're available online for less than $15. You can also cut and pit your cherries by hand, but I'll be honest: It's a pain in the behind, and your fingers might cramp from removing the pesky pits. And if you're one of those people who doesn't enjoy arugula, no worries! You can replace it with baby spinach or a tender leafy green mix instead.

½ cup (120 ml) Roasted Cherry Balsamic Vinaigrette (page 223), plus more to taste

4 ounces (115 g) arugula

½ English cucumber, thinly sliced

1 cup (160 g) fresh cherries, pitted and cut in half (about 12)

Freshly ground black pepper

1. Pour the vinaigrette into the base of a large bowl, then add the arugula, cucumber, and ¾ cup (120 g) of the cherries. Toss until the vinaigrette is evenly distributed throughout the salad.

2. Divide the salad evenly between serving plates, then top with the remaining cherries and a crack of black pepper. Serve immediately.

watermelon and basil salad with cucumber and maldon salt

Watermelon, basil, and cucumber? Sounds like an unlikely combination, but don't knock it till ya try it. Juicy watermelon actually pairs perfectly with crunchy cucumber and spicy basil to create a sweet-but-not-too-sweet salad. A squeeze of lemon juice and a healthy sprinkle of sea salt only help to enhance all of these flavors and take things to the next level.

A few notes on ingredients: Try to refrigerate your watermelon for at least four hours before making this recipe, as it is much better chilled. If you can't find Persian cucumbers near you, half of an American or English cucumber will work, too. And finally, I know Maldon salt is a little pricy, but one container will last you a long time and is so dang worth it—nothing quite compares to those thin and flaky crystals! Plus, you can also use it on "Everything" Avocado Toast (page 23) and Salted Caramel Chocolate Chip Cookies (page 198).

---

1 personal seedless watermelon, chilled

2 Persian cucumbers, thinly sliced

1 tablespoon thinly sliced fresh basil

Juice of ¼ lemon (1 to ½ teaspoons)

Maldon salt

1. Cut the rind off the watermelon and use a melon baller to create bite-size balls (or simply dice it). Put the melon in a large bowl with the cucumbers and basil, then gently toss to combine.

2. Divide the salad between serving plates, then top each with a squeeze of fresh lemon juice and generous sprinkle of Maldon salt. Serve immediately.

note: Swap the fresh basil for mint for a fun twist!

Hands-on time:	Cook time:	Serves 4 as a side,
15 MINUTES	30 MINUTES	2 as a main

chimichurri quinoa salad

In college I spent five months abroad in Buenos Aires, Argentina. It was certainly a life-changing experience, and I attribute most of my love of travel to the time I spent there. While most of the staple foods in *porteño* culture are not very vegan-friendly, there are a few hidden gems that I love and enjoy. One of them is chimichurri, an herbaceous, flavor-packed sauce of fresh herbs and garlic.

Chimichurri is most commonly served with meat, but here I use it as a dressing in a plant-centric salad. Nutty quinoa and roasted sweet potatoes both highlight and balance the boldness of the chimichurri, while Castelvetrano olives provide a nice buttery bite. This salad would be great for meal prep: (1) It won't wilt in the fridge, and (2) the flavor profile only improves over time as all the ingredients sit and mingle. If you'd like to bulk it up, you can easily toss it with some leafy greens, or top it with some diced avocado for an extra element of creaminess. Just make sure to use a mandoline to thinly slice the shallot; otherwise its flavor will be overpowering.

---

1 large sweet potato

1 cup (190 g) uncooked quinoa

½ cup (60 g) Castelvetrano olives, sliced

1 small shallot, thinly sliced

1 batch Chimichurri Dressing (page 224)

Salt and freshly ground black pepper

1. Preheat the oven to 400°F (205°C) and line a small baking sheet with parchment paper.

2. While the oven preheats, peel and dice the sweet potato and cook the quinoa according to its package instructions.

3. Place the sweet potato pieces in the center of the baking sheet; don't spread them out too much, or they will dry out in the oven. Bake on the middle rack of the oven for 30 minutes, flip with a spatula, then return to the oven for an additional 10 minutes.

4. Fluff the cooked quinoa with a fork, then add it to a large bowl with the roasted sweet potatoes, olives, shallot, and dressing. Toss together until everything is evenly coated in the dressing, then season with salt and pepper to taste. Serve warm or chilled; leftovers will keep in the fridge for up to 5 days.

curried chickpea salad

Save the chickens: Eat chickpeas instead! This salad makes a perfect packed lunch: It's full of fiber, protein, and healthy fats; it's quick to make; and it'll keep well for several days in the fridge. I'm a textural eater, and this one ticks all the boxes—soft chickpeas, crunchy veggies, and plump, juicy raisins in a creamy dressing. Each bite is a little different, which is just the way I like it!

Feel free to serve the salad however you please. I've provided a serving suggestion for an open-faced sandwich, but I've also enjoyed this on rice cakes, in wraps, stuffed into lettuce cups, or straight out of the Mason jar.

FOR THE CHICKPEA SALAD:

½ cup (120 ml) Cashew Cream (page 211)

Juice of 1 lemon (1 to 2 tablespoons)

2 teaspoons nutritional yeast

2½ teaspoons curry powder

½ teaspoon garlic powder

½ teaspoon cayenne pepper (optional)

1 teaspoon pink Himalayan salt

Freshly ground black pepper

4 cups (745 g) salt-free cooked chickpeas

¼ cup (45 g) raisins

1 carrot, peeled and shredded

1 cup (60 g) broccoli florets, finely chopped

2 green onions, thinly sliced

FOR SERVING (PER PERSON):

2 pieces gluten-free sourdough

Small handful of baby spinach

Freshly ground black pepper

1. Make the chickpea salad: Put the cashew cream, lemon juice, nutritional yeast, curry powder, garlic powder, cayenne, salt, and black pepper in a large bowl; mix until evenly combined. Add the chickpeas to the bowl and use a fork or potato masher to roughly mash half of the chickpeas. When they are mashed to your liking, stir them into the dressing and mix until evenly coated.

2. Fold the raisins, carrot, broccoli, and green onions into the chickpea mixture. Let sit for at least 15 minutes before serving as desired (for example, in a sandwich with spinach and more black pepper to taste); store leftovers in the fridge for up to 5 days.

mediterranean white bean salad

Creamy white beans stand in for feta cheese in this Greek-inspired salad. Olive brine, lemon juice, and nutritional yeast make a unique marinade that coats our legumes and veggies in vibrant, tangy flavor. Toss in some crunchy romaine, serve, and enjoy!

I munch on this salad as a light lunch, but you could also bulk it up with some cooked quinoa or another grain for a more filling dinner. If you're not a fan of romaine lettuce, arugula or a tender leafy green mix will work well here too. For an extra cheesy flavor, marinate your beans in the vinaigrette overnight before adding the remaining ingredients the following day.

¼ cup (60 ml) Kalamata olive brine

Juice of 1 lemon (1 to 2 tablespoons)

2 teaspoons nutritional yeast

½ teaspoon onion powder

2 tablespoons finely chopped fresh parsley

2 cups (360 g) cooked salt-free navy, cannellini, or great northern beans

1 cup (180 g) cherry tomatoes, cut in half

½ cup (70 g) pitted Kalamata olives, cut in half

½ English cucumber, diced

1 head of romaine lettuce, thinly sliced

1. Whisk the olive brine, lemon juice, nutritional yeast, onion powder, and parsley together in a large bowl. Add the beans, tomatoes, olives, and cucumber to the bowl, then toss to coat them with the dressing. Let marinate for at least 10 minutes, to allow all of the flavors to combine.

2. Fold in the lettuce, divide between plates, and serve immediately.

rosemary potato salad

This potato salad is an upgraded, adult-ified twist on the classic picnic fare. Make sure to finely (and I mean finely!) chop all of the herbs and grate your garlic. Large chunks of rosemary and thyme can be rather bitter, but they mellow out considerably when mixed with the creamy dressing. It's usually acceptable to swap dried herbs out for fresh, but I wouldn't recommend it here. Fresh herbs have a more complex flavor profile, and their dried varieties won't rehydrate well or add much flavor. You'll have extra of both herbs, so I suggest making some Butternut Bean Bisque (page 72) or Lentil-Quinoa Stew (page 76) to use them up.

FOR THE POTATO SALAD:

- 2 pounds (905 g) small gold or red potatoes, cut into 1-inch (2.5 cm) pieces
- 1 teaspoon pink Himalayan salt
- 2 ribs celery, finely diced (heaping ¼ cup, 45 g)

FOR THE ROSEMARY DRESSING:

- ½ cup (120 ml) Cashew Mayo (page 211)
- 1 tablespoon Dijon mustard
- 1 tablespoon apple cider vinegar
- 1 teaspoon nutritional yeast
- 1 clove garlic, finely grated with a Microplane
- ½ teaspoon finely chopped fresh rosemary
- ½ teaspoon finely chopped fresh thyme
- ½ teaspoon freshly ground black pepper
- ¼ teaspoon pink Himalayan salt, plus more to taste

1. Make the potato salad: Put the potatoes and salt in a large pot and fill with water until the potatoes are just covered. Cover and bring to a boil over high heat. When the water starts to boil, remove the lid, reduce the heat to medium-high, and cook for 7 to 8 minutes, until the potatoes are tender. Drain the potatoes and immediately rinse them with cold water to stop them from cooking further.

2. While the potatoes are cooking, make the rosemary dressing: Put the vegan mayo, mustard, vinegar, nutritional yeast, garlic, rosemary, thyme, pepper, and salt in a large bowl and mix well. Add the celery and cooked potatoes, then fold them into the dressing until coated. Season with additional salt to taste, if necessary.

3. Place in the fridge for at least 15 minutes, to cool and allow the flavors to combine, before serving. Serve chilled; leftovers will keep in the fridge for up to 5 days.

purple power slaw

This slaw may look simple, but don't be fooled—it packs a powerful flavor punch. Not only is purple cabbage a great source of antioxidants and vitamins A, C, and B_6, but it also serves as the perfect crunchy vessel for our spicy marinade of ginger, garlic, and lime juice. A touch of cashew cream adds some healthy fats and balances out the acidity to make this slaw absolutely addicting. Seriously, sometimes I can eat (and have eaten) a giant bowl of this as an afternoon snack! If you're not as crazy as me, it's also great with practically any Asian-style dish—like Sheet Pan Teriyaki Bowls (page 171), Garlicky Green Bean Stir-Fry with Sticky Orange Tempeh (page 165), or Pineapple Unfried Rice (page 162). It's honestly hard to go wrong with this stuff—it's also great on sandwiches, tacos, stuffed into burritos, or simply as a nice textural contrast alongside steamed vegetables.

Make sure to finely grate both the garlic and ginger for this recipe using a Microplane—we're using them raw, so you don't want any huge chunks. If you're sensitive to spice, cut the amounts of both in half and go from there. The cabbage in this recipe should also be shredded as thinly as possible, preferably with a mandoline. This makes it much more satisfying to eat, and it doesn't have to sit for long to fully marinate.

Juice of 1 lime

1 large clove garlic, finely grated with a Microplane

½-inch (12 mm) knob of fresh ginger, peeled and finely grated with a Microplane

2 tablespoons Cashew Cream (page 211)

½ teaspoon pink Himalayan salt

½ large head of red cabbage, thinly sliced with a mandoline

1. Put the lime juice, garlic, ginger, cashew cream, and salt in the base of a large bowl and mix well. Add the cabbage and toss to coat with the marinade.

2. Let the slaw sit for at least 10 minutes before serving as desired; leftovers will keep in the fridge for up to 5 days, but will soften over time.

dijon brussels slaw

Whether you're serving it as a picnic side or topping for veggie burgers, this slaw packs a unique flavor punch! Instead of using my classic cashew-based mayo to make things creamy, this slaw relies on a Dijon tahini sauce, which also makes it a great nut-free side to share with guests. Freshly chopped apples bring a sweet and tart flavor contrast, while just a touch of apple cider vinegar gives the slaw some brightness and acidity.

Brussels sprouts can be enjoyed raw, as long as you finely shred them. That being said, you will need to use the thinnest setting on your mandoline for this recipe. Please be careful and use a protective glove or the safety device, though—these sprouts are small, and you can easily nick your finger. If you want to cut down on the prep time, you can also buy pre-shredded sprouts at your grocery store.

1   cup (240 ml) Tahini Dijon Sauce (page 212)

2   tablespoons apple cider vinegar

5   cups (580 g) trimmed and finely shredded Brussels sprouts

½   Granny Smith apple, peeled and cut into matchsticks

Salt and freshly ground black pepper

1. Whisk the sauce and vinegar together in the base of a medium bowl until well combined. Add the Brussels sprouts and apple, then mix until everything is evenly coated in sauce.

2. Season with salt and pepper to taste, then store in the fridge for at least 15 minutes before serving. Leftovers will keep in the fridge for up to 5 days.

5 | grab and go

If you see me out in public, odds are that I will have a snack on hand. Hanger is pretty much the worst thing ever, so I always travel prepared, just in case! Store-bought snacks are definitely convenient, but are often made with funky preservatives or questionable ingredients—not to mention that all of that packaging adds up, really fast. Here are a few of my favorite homemade snacks that I munch on throughout the day. Some are sweet and others are savory, but all are super yummy and nutritious.

all-in-one sushi

one-bowl banana bread balls

You know those days when you really want a slice of banana bread, but can't be bothered to turn on your oven? That's when you make these! Buttery walnuts, quick-cooking oats, vanilla, and cinnamon give them that classic banana bread flavor we all know and love. Chewy, doughy, and perfectly spiced, they're a great afternoon snack or a midday treat for your little ones. I'll even eat a couple for dessert when the mood strikes . . . but—full disclosure—I usually top them with some peanut butter.

These balls lean more toward the subtly sweet side, which is just the way I like 'em. If you have a bigger sweet tooth, however, add 1 extra tablespoon maple syrup to sweeten the deal. Oh, and if you do have time to bake, you should totally make my Fluffy Banana Bread (page 27).

2	cups (210 g) quick-cooking oats
1½	cups (165 g) walnuts
1	large ripe banana
1	tablespoon grade A maple syrup
2	teaspoons vanilla extract
2	teaspoons ground cinnamon
¼	teaspoon pink Himalayan salt

1. Put the oats and walnuts in a food processor and process for 45 seconds, until a fine flour forms. Roughly break up the banana into bite-size chunks and add it to the food processor, along with the maple syrup, vanilla, cinnamon, and salt. Pulse until everything is evenly combined, then place the dough in the fridge for 10 minutes to allow the dough to set.

2. When the dough is firm, slightly wet your hands and roll out balls with the dough, using a 2-tablespoon scoop for each ball. Store leftovers in the fridge for up to 7 days, or keep in the freezer for up to 1 month.

note: Make sure your banana is brown and spotty—just like you would for banana bread! Otherwise it won't be sweet enough.

the best hummus...ever

Ever wonder how to make hummus the "right" way? As in, ending up with a version that's so perfectly smooth, creamy, and rich that you'll never want to even look at a tub of the store-bought stuff again? You only need five ingredients to make this mind-blowing recipe, but it delivers big in the texture and flavor departments.

One of the keys to making incredibly creamy hummus is to cook dried chickpeas from scratch—canned just won't cut it here, folks. Soaking the beans in advance and cooking them in an Instant Pot turns the cook time into practically nothing, but you can also cook them on the stovetop in a pinch. The other trick is to remove the peels from the cooked chickpeas. The hummus-making process can be a long one, but the good news is that it makes a big batch, and it's pretty mindless in and of itself. So turn on your favorite podcast, TV show, or the latest Netflix craze and cook, peel, and process away! You'll end up with a superior slather-it-on-everything end result that can be dressed up with any toppings you love. My personal favorites are smoked paprika, cumin, and za'atar, a deeply flavored Middle Eastern spice with lots of dried thyme and sesame seeds.

---

12   ounces (340 g) dried chickpeas (about 2 cups), soaked in water for 12 hours

3 to 5   cloves garlic, peeled (use more if you're a garlic lover)

1   teaspoon baking soda

Juice of 1 lemon (1 to 2 tablespoons)

1½   teaspoons pink Himalayan salt

¾   cup (190 g) tahini

1   cup (240 ml) water, placed in the freezer for 15 minutes

Toppings, as desired

1. Drain and rinse the soaked chickpeas, then add them to an Instant Pot or a large pot, along with the garlic and baking soda.

2. For the Instant Pot (recommended): Add enough water to cover the chickpeas by 2 to 3 inches (5 to 7.5 cm), then close the pot and set the valve to sealing. Cook on Manual High pressure for 10 to 12 minutes; let the pressure naturally release for 10 minutes, then move the valve from sealing to venting to release the remaining pressure.

3. For the stovetop: Add enough water to cover the chickpeas by

3 to 5 inches (7.5 to 12 cm). Bring to a boil over medium-high heat and cook until the beans are tender, 40 to 120 minutes.

4. Drain and rinse the cooked beans until no bubbles remain. Set the garlic aside and peel the chickpeas by pinching them between your fingers—the skins should slide off easily. Discard the chickpea skins, or better yet, chuck 'em in your compost.

5. Put the peeled chickpeas and garlic in the bowl of a food processor and begin to process. Mix the lemon juice and salt together in a small bowl, then add

this mixture to the food processor as it is running. Process until the mixture is smooth, pausing to scrape the sides of the bowl with a spatula as necessary.

6. Add ½ cup (125 g) of the tahini to the food processor, then close the device and begin to process. Pour ⅓ cup (75 ml)

ice-cold water into the device as it is running; let the processor continue to run for 4 to 5 minutes, to help make the hummus fluffy and smooth. If you would like your spread to be thicker or creamier, add the remaining tahini and water in ¼-cup (60 ml) increments.

7. Top the hummus as desired, then serve. Leftovers will keep in an airtight container in the fridge for up to 5 days.

note: The quality of your tahini will make a huge difference here, so go with the best you can find.

baked oatmeal bars

I loved granola bars as a kid. Well, at least I thought I did. Looking back, I think those chocolate-covered, sugar-filled rectangles of peanut-buttery, chocolate-chip goodness would qualify more as candy bars than granola bars. These oatmeal bars are inspired by the "granola" bars of my childhood, but with a few healthier twists. First, we'll skip the refined white table sugar and sweeten these babies with some gooey Medjool dates and maple syrup. I've also swapped the classic combination of rolled oats and puffed rice for steel-cut oatmeal, which provides both a chewy softness and crunchier bite all in one go.

Mini chocolate chips still add a touch of nostalgia and fun to these bars, but you can replace them with cacao nibs or finely chopped fruit, nuts, or seeds if you're looking for something made from entirely whole-food ingredients. And speaking of nuts, you can easily replace the peanut butter with sunflower butter or tahini if you have an allergy. Finally, I've noticed that a lot of blenders have problems blending Medjool dates smoothly. Blending them with a small amount of liquid before adding the rest of the ingredients helps to get rid of those pesky chunks.

⅓ packed cup (95 g) Medjool dates, pitted

1 cup (240 ml) unsweetened nondairy milk

⅓ cup (75 ml) maple syrup

½ cup (120 g) creamy peanut butter

1 teaspoon vanilla extract

2 cups (260 g) steel-cut oats

¼ cup (55 g) mini dairy-free chocolate chips

1. Preheat the oven to 325°F (165°C) and line a 9-inch (23 cm) square baking pan with parchment paper.

2. Put the dates in a high-speed blender with ½ cup (120 ml) of the milk and blend until a smooth paste forms, 30 to 45 seconds. Add the remaining milk, the maple syrup, peanut butter, and vanilla to the blender and process until smooth. Finally, add the oats and chocolate chips to the blender and blend on low speed to mix them into the batter. If your blender does not have a low speed, transfer the wet mixture to a bowl and use a spatula to fold everything together.

3. Transfer the batter to the baking pan and bake on the middle rack of the oven for 45 minutes. Let sit in the pan for 5 minutes, then transfer the parchment paper-lined bars to a wire rack to cool completely before slicing into 10 bars.

4. Leftovers will keep at room temperature for up to 3 days, or in the fridge for up to 1 week.

pumpkin spice date bites

I like to call these little grain- and nut-free energy balls "bites of fall happiness." They have a wholesome, naturally sweetened base of caramel-y dates, raisins, and warming fall spices that encases a blend of pumpkin, sunflower, hemp, and chia seeds. Most bite recipes involve blending everything together to get a more uniform consistency, but I kept all of the crunchy ingredients whole here for some extra texture. Plus, it's been scientifically proven that you feel more satiated after chewing your food (which is why eating whole fruit, for example, is often better than sipping on a smoothie).

Whether you enjoy a bite with your morning coffee or pack a couple as an afternoon snack, these fun balls will provide you with sustainable (and delicious!) energy to get your ish done. They're also a great source of healthy fats, fiber, and protein! If you already have a pumpkin pie spice blend in your pantry, skip the blend of spices here and use 2 teaspoons of that instead.

½   packed cup (115 g) Medjool dates, pitted

¼   cup (50 g) raisins

1   cup (240 ml) hot water

1   teaspoon ground cinnamon

½   teaspoon ground ginger

¼   teaspoon grated nutmeg

¼   teaspoon ground cloves

¼   teaspoon pink Himalayan salt

1   cup (135 g) hulled pumpkin seeds (pepitas)

1   cup (120 g) sunflower seeds

½   cup (90 g) chia seeds

¼   cup (35 g) hemp hearts

1. Put the dates and raisins in a bowl and cover with the hot water. Let everything soak for 5 minutes, then drain, saving the water. Put the soaked fruit in a food processor with the cinnamon, ginger, nutmeg, cloves, salt, and ¼ cup (60 ml) of the soaking water. Process until a thick, uniform paste forms, adding more water as necessary.

2. Use a spatula to transfer the fruit and spice paste to a medium bowl, then add the pumpkin seeds, sunflower seeds, chia seeds, and hemp hearts. Fold the seed mixture into the date mixture until evenly incorporated,

then refrigerate for 15 minutes, to allow the dough to thicken.

3. Slightly wet your hands, then scoop 2 heaping tablespoons of dough into your hands and gently press and roll into a ball. Repeat with the remaining mixture; if things start to stick to your hands, rinse them off and re-dampen them.

4. Place the finished energy bites in the fridge, where they will keep for up to 10 days.

> **note:** Save the rest of the water used to soak the dates and raisins for smoothies or tea—it has a lovely caramel flavor!

green curry cashews

I always seem to have a half-used jar of curry paste sitting in my fridge, and never really knew what to do with it . . . until I had the brilliant idea for these cashews! This flavor-packed combination of cashews, coconut flakes, and sesame seeds is the perfect crunchy, salty, and savory snack, especially when those midafternoon cravings hit. I also love to whip up a batch when entertaining friends in place of the sad bowl of plain roasted nuts that nobody really wants to eat. While this recipe will keep at room temperature for up to five days, it will soften with time, so if you like things crispy, gobble them up immediately! Finally, try to find larger coconut flakes, not coconut shreds; the shreds are too small and will burn quickly in the oven.

- 2 tablespoons Thai green curry paste
- 2 teaspoons tamari
- 2 teaspoons maple syrup
- ½ teaspoon grated lime zest
- 1 cup (145 g) raw cashews
- ⅓ cup (15 g) unsweetened coconut flakes (not shreds)
- 1 tablespoon sesame seeds

1. Preheat the oven to 325°F (165°C) and line a baking sheet with parchment paper or a reusable silicone mat.

2. Put the curry paste, tamari, maple syrup, and lime zest in a medium bowl, then mix everything together to form a thick paste.

3. Add the cashews, coconut flakes, and sesame seeds to the bowl and mix until everything is evenly coated. Spread the nut mixture evenly across the baking sheet.

4. Bake on the bottom rack of the oven for 5 minutes, then remove the pan and stir the nuts. Repeat this process two more times, cooking the nuts for 15 minutes total.

5. Serve immediately, or store leftovers in an airtight container at room temperature for up to 5 days.

note: This recipe will also work with a red or yellow curry paste—green is just my personal favorite.

no-bake cosmic brownies

While there are no rainbow chocolate chips in this recipe, I still think these brownies are out of this world. Puns aside, this six-ingredient snack is a healthier take on one of my favorite lunchbox staples. I don't know how the combination of sticky dates, almond butter, vanilla extract, and buckwheat flour combine to create an eerily similar but totally good-for-you treat, but I'm not gonna complain. Never heard of buckwheat flour? No worries—it's available in most grocery stores and is totally gluten-free, despite it's confusing name. Fun fact: it's actually a seed! Cacao powder is typically raw and goes through a different process than cocoa—it has a sweeter, less bitter taste that means the recipe needs less sugar overall.

These no-bake brownies are firm enough to wrap up and pack in a lunchbox, and won't melt with excessive heat. They're an awesome midday snack, but are equally enjoyable for dessert. If you're feeling adventurous, try crumbling one over some vegan ice cream or pulsing it into a dairy-free milkshake!

---

1   packed cup (220 g) Medjool dates, pitted

¼   cup (65 g) unsalted almond butter

1   teaspoon vanilla extract

¾   cup (95 g) buckwheat flour

½   cup (45 g) cacao powder

¼   teaspoon pink Himalayan salt

⅓   cup (75 g) mini dairy-free chocolate chips

note: Nut allergy? You can replace the almond butter with tahini or sunflower butter, though it will affect the final taste. You can also swap it out with some peanut butter for some PB brownie goodness!

1. Put the pitted dates in a bowl and cover them with hot water. Set aside and let soak for 5 minutes, then drain well. Put the dates in a food processor with the almond butter and vanilla; process for 30 seconds, or until a smooth paste forms.

2. Add the buckwheat flour, cacao powder, and salt to the food processor. Blend for 45 to 60 seconds, until a thick, even batter forms. If your batter is too dry, add water in 1-tablespoon increments until it is smooth and fudgy. Set 2 tablespoons of the chocolate chips aside, then add the rest to the food processor and pulse into the batter until evenly combined.

3. Line a 9 by 4-inch (10 by 23 cm) loaf pan with waxed paper or parchment paper, then transfer the brownie batter to the pan. Use a spatula to firmly and evenly press the batter into the pan. Sprinkle on the remaining chocolate chips, then gently press them into the batter. Place in the fridge for 10 to 15 minutes, to allow the mixture to set. Remove from the pan and use a sharp knife to cut the brownies into 8 equal pieces. Serve as desired; store leftovers in an airtight container at room temperature for up to 5 days.

Hands-on time:
30 MINUTES

Cook time:
45 MINUTES

Serves 1 or 2 as a main,
3 or 4 as a snack

all-in-one sushi

I loooove sushi. It's an easy (and filling) way to get in some healthy carbs and veggies while still feeling light and energized. I also think it's the perfect grab-and-go meal—except for the fact that you need a separate container for your dipping sauce and wasabi. This "all-in-one" sushi solves that problem, though, by pre-seasoning the rice with all of your favorite add-ins!

If you end up making this sushi often, try switching up the veggies for increased variety. I love to add some roasted sweet potato, bell pepper, and/or enoki mushrooms when I'm feeling fancy. Also, a bamboo mat is not essential to sushi making, but it sure does make it easier. Most grocery stores sell them in the $3 to $5 range, so it's a pretty affordable investment.

FOR THE SEASONED RICE:

- 1½ cups (280 g) short-grain brown rice
- ¾ teaspoon garlic powder
- ¾ teaspoon ground ginger
- 2 tablespoons tamari
- 1 tablespoon black sesame seeds
- 4 teaspoons unseasoned rice vinegar

FOR THE SUSHI:

- 4 sheets nori
- 1 small carrot, peeled and cut into matchsticks
- ¼ English cucumber, peeled and cut into matchsticks
- 4 ounces (115 g) store-bought seasoned tofu, sliced
- ½ avocado, thinly sliced

1. Make the seasoned rice: Put the rice, garlic powder, ginger, and tamari in a medium pot with 2⅔ cups (630 ml) water. Bring to a boil over high heat, then cover, reduce the heat to low, and simmer for 45 minutes. Immediately remove the lid from the pot and add the sesame seeds and vinegar; stir well, then transfer to a larger bowl and let cool while you prepare the sushi fillings.

2. Roll your sushi: Place the nori shiny side down on a bamboo rolling mat, then use a spatula to firmly press rice all over its surface, leaving a ½-inch (12 mm) space at the top. When the rice is evenly spread, place a small portion of the carrot, cucumber, tofu, and avocado in a straight line across the bottom third of the roll—be careful not to overfill it!

3. Grab the underside of the bamboo mat and roll the sushi away from you, making sure to press firmly. Fold the excess portion of the mat toward you as you continue to roll the sushi; when you reach the top of the roll, use your fingers to spread some water across the bare strip of nori. Press the roll into the strip to seal the roll, then transfer to a cutting board and cut crosswise with a sharp or serrated knife.

4. Repeat for the remaining rolls, until you run out of rice and fillings. Serve as desired; leftovers will keep in the fridge for up to 3 days.

low-waste kitchen hacks

Have you heard of the zero-waste movement? It's a totally rad initiative that aims to completely eliminate all unnecessary waste from our lives. Every piece of plastic that has ever been created still exists on this planet today; when you think about all of those takeout containers, cartons of almond milk, or even tubs of salad greens you've bought, that can *really* add up.

I'm constantly trying to reduce my waste, but I am by no means perfect—I'm human, after all! That's why I prefer to use the phrase *low waste* over *zero waste*. I'm pretty sure the only way to live completely waste-free would be to cut yourself off from society, live in a forest, and only survive off of naturally growing berries and veggies. Let's face it: There is *no way* that's gonna happen.

Luckily for you and me, progress is the new perfection. Every small step you take toward reducing your waste is a big one, in my book! Here are some of my top tips and personal practices for reducing waste in the kitchen.

BYOB: Bags, that is! Minimizing your waste starts *before* you even get to the store. I bought a set of reusable tote bags and produce bags online ages ago, and they still work to this day. Some stores will even give you a discount when you bring your own bag! I keep mine in the trunk of my car, so I never have to worry about forgetting them. Also, don't forget to wash your produce bags every once in a while—both you and the cashier will be much, much happier.

Shop in bulk: Not only is it more eco-friendly, but it's more cost-effective as well! This goes for produce as well as dried goods. I try to always buy my leafy greens, carrots, celery, and potatoes in bulk—most stores sell them plastic-free, and you also get to take home only what you need. Dried goods can be a little trickier depending on where you live, but if you have a grocery store with a bulk section, don't be afraid to check it out! Sometimes you can bring your own containers and fill them, or you can simply reuse the plastic bags the store offers. And don't forget to take a picture of the item number with your phone, so you don't have to use the twist ties.

Opt for glass: When I can't find something I need in the bulk bins, I try to purchase it in either a glass jar or recyclable packaging. Single-use plastic is *so* 2015, plus you can reuse your jars! Nut butter jars make the perfect container for overnight oats, and I save larger jars (like pasta sauce jars) to store granola, dinner leftovers, and dried goods I bought in bulk.

"Invest" in kitchenware: Food-grade silicone (which is rubber, not plastic) has been a total game-changer in the kitchen for me. I kid you not when I say that I use my silicone baking mats daily! Silicone muffin tins, donut pans, and even popsicle molds are both nonstick and reusable. They're pretty affordable, and when you think about it, buying one item once saves you way more money in the long run than buying single-use products, repeatedly, forever. There are some situations where silicone just won't work (like lining a baking pan)—I always keep a roll of unbleached, partially recycled parchment paper on hand for that.

Store smart: Invest in a good set of glass storage containers, or just use those leftover glass jars I talked about earlier. I'd also recommend ditching those single-use sealable bags and purchasing some reusable silicone ones instead. They seal just as well, work in the fridge and freezer, and are totally dishwasher safe.

Follow the 5 Rs, in order: Refuse what you don't need. Reduce what you use. Reuse what you can. Recycle the leftovers. Rot (compost) the rest. I'd like to say I came up with that myself, but it's a pretty common saying in the low-waste movement.

6 | extra crispy

One of my favorite kitchen tools to play around with is my air fryer. If you've never heard of it before, it's essentially a fun-size countertop convection oven that crisps food beautifully and evenly—without the need for any added oil! At first I didn't believe the air-fryer hype (I mean, I already have an oven), but as soon as I got one, I was hooked. It's great for small-batch cooking *and* for reheating leftovers without that soggy, chewy microwave effect. I'd definitely say it's worth the counter space, but if you don't own one yet, no worries! All of these recipes can be made in a regular oven as well, with a few modifications.

golden cauliflower wings

stupid easy croutons

You know what has always annoyed me? That practically every version of store-bought croutons has dairy in it! I had pretty much given up finding suitable crispy, bread-based salad toppings after I ditched dairy, but totally gave up after going mostly gluten-free . . . until I decided to make my own in my air fryer! The air fryer evenly crisps the croutons and achieves this beautiful golden-brown color, without the need for any added oil. You can also make these croutons in the oven, but that uniform consistency is a bit trickier to achieve.

This recipe is pretty simple: Dice your bread, coat it in a touch of water to help some seasonings stick, then bake until crispy. I've provided three different crouton variations below, all of which are great on both soups and salads. After you've tested them out, I encourage you to get creative and use your own favorite combination of spices.

FOR PLAIN JANE CROUTONS:

- 2 cups (120 g) gluten-free bread cut into ½-inch (12 mm) cubes
- Pinch of pink Himalayan or sea salt

FOR CHEESY GARLIC CROUTONS:

- 1 tablespoon nutritional yeast
- ½ teaspoon garlic powder

FOR "EVERYTHING" CROUTONS:

- ½ teaspoon onion powder
- ¼ teaspoon garlic powder
- 1 teaspoon sesame seeds
- 1 teaspoon poppy seeds

FOR LEMON PEPPER CROUTONS:

- ½ teaspoon grated lemon zest
- ½ teaspoon freshly ground black pepper

1. Put the bread in a large bowl. Drizzle 2 teaspoons water over the bread, then add the salt and any additional seasonings (if desired). Toss until well combined.

2. Transfer the bread cubes to the basket of an air fryer and bake at 360°F (180°C) for 7 to 8 minutes, shaking the basket halfway through. Let cool slightly, then serve as desired. Leftovers will keep at room temperature for up to 5 days.

note: Oven option: Line a baking sheet with parchment paper or a silicone mat, spread the bread cubes over it, and bake at 360°F (180°C) for 15 to 18 minutes.

crispy seasoned chickpeas

If you haven't made crispy chickpeas before, you're kind of missing out. Not only are they a great crouton alternative for salads (page 80), but they're also a tasty on-the-go snack on their own. Nowadays there are a lot of store-bought versions of crispy chickpeas, but they're often made with oil and extra preservatives. I like to skip all of that and make my own at home—they're just as delicious, easily customizable, and much less expensive.

I coat my chickpeas in a savory, smoky seasoning blend, but these chickpeas will crisp up with whatever spices you put on them, so get creative! Italian seasoning, taco seasoning, curry spices, or even sweeter spices like cinnamon will work beautifully—just make sure the chickpeas are well coated and not too wet before you place them in your air fryer. If you are using canned chickpeas that contain salt, omit the salt from this recipe.

2   cups (325 g) cooked salt-free chickpeas

1   tablespoon nutritional yeast

½   teaspoon smoked paprika

½   teaspoon garlic powder

½   teaspoon pink Himalayan salt

¼   teaspoon cayenne pepper (optional)

1. Put the chickpeas in a medium bowl, then sprinkle the nutritional yeast, smoked paprika, garlic powder, salt, and cayenne (if using) over the top. Use a spatula to fold the spices into the chickpeas; when everything is evenly coated, transfer the chickpeas to the base of the basket of an air fryer.

2. Bake the chickpeas at 350°F (175°C) for 20 minutes, removing the basket and shaking the chickpeas every 5 minutes. Let cool completely before storing in an airtight container at room temperature for up to 3 days.

note: Oven option: Line a baking sheet with parchment paper or a silicone mat, spread the seasoned chickpeas over it, and bake at 400°F (205°C) for 35 to 40 minutes, tossing once halfway through.

maple-glazed brussels sprouts

Is it just me, or did childhood cartoons totally ruin Brussels sprouts for you? I wasn't a picky kid, by any means, but I always avoided them because of the moans and complaints my favorite animated characters would give every time a grouchy old lunch lady ladled them onto their plate. Thank goodness I finally came to my senses and gave them a try!

Now, Brussels sprouts can be bland and soggy, especially if you boil them or buy them frozen. However, when you use fresh sprouts and roast them to crunchy perfection? I could snack on that all day, every day. Here I coat them in a simple combination of smoked paprika, maple syrup, and tamari for some smoky, sweet, and savory goodness. Even if your air fryer has a nonstick basket, I recommend lining it with a small piece of parchment paper to prevent sticking. I've also provided an oven option for this recipe, but I will note that the air fryer crisps up this cruciferous veggie more evenly—and in almost half the time!

---

3 cups (330 g) Brussels sprouts

1 tablespoon tamari

1 tablespoon maple syrup

¼ teaspoon smoked paprika

¼ teaspoon pink Himalayan salt

1. Line the basket of an air fryer with parchment paper. Wash, trim, and cut the Brussels sprouts in half. Whisk the tamari, maple syrup, smoked paprika, and salt together in a medium bowl, then add the Brussels sprouts. Toss until evenly coated, then transfer to the air fryer.

2. Bake at 400°F (205°C) for 17 to 20 minutes, removing the basket to shake the sprouts every 5 minutes. Serve immediately.

note: Oven option: Line a baking sheet with parchment paper or a silicone mat, spread the Brussel sprouts across it, and bake on the top rack of the oven at 425°F (220°C) for 30 to 35 minutes.

baby bella bites

There's a reason why I use mushrooms in so many of my "cozier" recipes. They have an incredible texture and rich, umami flavor that most plants seem to lack. Well, actually they're not a plant; as my dear friend Timmy likes to remind everyone, they are technically a fungi.

Regardless, these baby bella bites are juicy, flavor-filled, and oh so fun to pop in your mouth. They're a fun twist on the classic party app, but also easy enough to cook alongside your favorite dinner to mix into a salad. You can easily serve them as is, but it's always more fun to dip—dunking them in the leftover marinade makes them even yummier.

---

2   tablespoons low-sodium tamari

½   teaspoon freshly ground black pepper

½   teaspoon garlic powder

8   ounces (225 g) baby bella or cremini mushrooms, stems trimmed, cut in half

1. Combine the tamari, pepper, and garlic powder in a medium bowl. Add the mushrooms and use a spatula to toss them until they are evenly coated in the marinade. Let sit for 15 minutes, stirring once halfway through.

2. Transfer the mushrooms to the basket of an air fryer, but save the marinade. Bake at 400°F (205°C) for 10 to 12 minutes, shaking the basket every 3 minutes. Serve alongside leftover marinade as a dipping sauce, or as desired.

note: Oven option: Line a baking sheet with parchment paper or a silicone mat, spread the mushrooms over it, and bake on the top rack of the oven at 450°F (230°C) for 12 to 14 minutes, until golden and juicy.

cheesy battered zucchini fries

My boyfriend and I planted our first garden this summer, and innocently (ignorantly?) planted not one, not two, but three zucchini plants. Little did we know that those things grow to be huge and pretty much take over your garden. Needless to say, we have been enjoying a variety of zucchini dishes this summer, and luckily haven't tired of that long, green squash yet—partly because of these cheesy battered fries.

Chickpea flour, nutritional yeast, and garlic powder form the flavor trifecta of the glorious batter that coats these fun-size spears of zucchini. The air fryer crisps up the golden coating perfectly without drying it out, though I would suggest lining your basket with parchment paper to prevent sticking. These fries are quite tasty on their own, but are utterly mouthwatering when dunked in Rosemary Tahini Sauce.

---

1   zucchini

3   tablespoons chickpea flour (garbanzo bean flour)

1   tablespoon nutritional yeast

¼   teaspoon garlic powder

½   teaspoon pink Himalayan salt

3   tablespoons nondairy milk

Rosemary Tahini Sauce (page 212; optional), for dipping

note: Oven option: Line a baking sheet with parchment paper or a silicone mat, arrange the zucchini over it, and bake on the top rack of the oven at 450°F (230°C) for 15 minutes.

1. Line the basket of an air fryer with parchment paper. Rinse the zucchini, quarter it lengthwise, and cut each quarter into 2-inch (5 cm) spears. Pat the spears dry with a clean kitchen cloth, then set aside while you prepare the batter.

2. Put the chickpea flour, nutritional yeast, garlic powder, and salt in a small bowl. Mix until well combined, then pour in the milk and whisk until no clumps remain.

3. Dunk each piece of zucchini into the batter and gently shake any excess off. Carefully place each battered piece into the air fryer basket, making sure there is space between the pieces. (You may have to work in batches, depending on the size of your air fryer basket.) Bake at 400°F (205°C) for 15 minutes, then use a spatula to remove the fries from the air fryer.

4. Serve warm as is, or alongside tahini sauce.

golden cauliflower wings

If you've been to practically any vegan restaurant, odds are you've seen cauliflower "Buffalo wings" on the menu. These "wings" still have that crispy golden coating, but are air-fried instead of deep-fried for a lighter, but still satisfying, take.

Not only are these plant-based wings a fun appetizer to enjoy with friends, but they're also a great garnish: Use them to top Pineapple Unfried Rice (page 162) or Garlicky Green Bean Stir-Fry (page 165), for example. Feel free to replace the sauce with another wing sauce of your choosing. Buffalo and/or barbecue sauce would be absolutely great here, or just skip the sauce and serve them with a side of Jalapeño Ranch (page 232) for dunking.

Some tips for success: As with any two-step battering process, it's best to use separate hands when dunking the cauliflower in the wet and dry mixes. Even so, the dry mix tends to get a little wet and lumpy over time. Dividing the dry mix into two smaller bowls and swapping it out halfway through helps to keep things clean and tidy.

FOR THE WET MIX:

- ½ cup (60 g) brown rice flour
- ½ cup (150 ml) nondairy milk
- ½ teaspoon pink Himalayan salt

FOR THE DRY MIX:

- 1½ cups (140 g) blanched almond flour
- ½ teaspoon paprika
- 1 small head of cauliflower, cut into bite-sized florets
- ½ cup (120 ml) Healthy Orange Sauce (page 227) or Date-Sweetened Teriyaki Sauce (page 228), or a mix of both

1. Line the basket of an air fryer with parchment paper.

2. Make the wet mix: Put the brown rice flour, milk, and salt in a small bowl and whisk until no lumps remain.

3. Make the dry mix: In a separate, slightly larger bowl with a wide base, whisk the almond flour and paprika together.

4. Using one hand, dunk each cauliflower floret into the wet mix, shaking off any excess batter. Carefully transfer the floret into the bowl of the dry mix, using a separate hand to gently coat it in the almond flour mixture. Place the battered cauliflower in the basket and repeat with the remaining florets. Make sure to leave some space between them; otherwise they'll stick together. You will probably have to divide the florets into two batches, depending on the size of your basket.

5. Bake at 345°F (175°C) for 17 minutes, then carefully transfer the cauliflower florets to a large bowl. Drizzle half (or all, if all of the wings fit) of the sauce over them, then use a spatula to carefully coat them in the sauce.

Return to the air fryer basket and bake for an additional 5 to 7 minutes, then remove and serve immediately.

note: Oven option: Line a baking sheet with parchment paper or a silicone mat, arrange the battered cauliflower over it, and bake on the top rack of the oven at 475°F (245°C) for 10 minutes. Remove from the oven and use a spatula to flip, then bake for an additional 5 minutes. Remove once more, coat in sauce as directed, and bake for 5 minutes.

7 | quick and cozy

Just like the air fryer, the electric pressure cooker is one of those must-have countertop appliances. Long gone are the days of their finicky stovetop counterparts—or standing over a regular ol' pot for hours on end. Electric pressure cookers are fast, convenient, and a great way to make large quantities of food with minimal hands-on time and cleanup. (To avoid steam and splatter when you release the pressure, cover the valve with a dish towel.) There are several brands of pressure cookers on the market, all with pretty similar functions. I recommend the Instant Pot; my six-quart pot has been well used since my early college days, and hasn't failed me yet.

instant pot pumpkin pasta

pressure cooker bulk beans

One of my favorite ways to use my pressure cooker is to cook beans in bulk. Not only are they much more cost-effective than buying canned beans, but it's also so much easier to add fun flavors, control the salt level, and ditch some of those weird preservatives. I think you'll find that they simply taste better, too!

These recipes make quite a bit of cooked legumes; I use them for meal prep, either tossed in a salad or alongside a grain, roasted veggies, and a creamy dressing. For more serving suggestions, check out the "Let's Get Saucy" chapter (pages 208 to 235) for some inspo! A few more notes: You do not need to soak your beans ahead of time for these recipes (I usually forget), but if you do, there's an adjusted cooking time in each recipe. Second, don't completely drain your beans after you cook them—storing them in some of the cooking liquid prevents them from drying out and infuses them with extra flavor.

Hands-on time:	**Cook time:**	**Makes about 5 cups (860 g)**
5 MINUTES	35 MINUTES PLUS TIME TO COME TO PRESSURE	

chipotle lime pinto beans

- 2 cups (385 g) dried pinto beans
- ½ teaspoon grated lime zest
- 2 teaspoons chipotle chile powder (pure chipotle, not a blend of spices)
- Juice of 1 lime
- 1 teaspoon pink Himalayan salt

1. Put the beans, lime zest, chile powder, and 6 cups (1.4 L) water in a pressure cooker. Close the Instant Pot, set the valve to sealing, and cook on Manual High pressure for 35 minutes. (If you soaked your beans, drain and rinse them, and then put them in the pressure cooker for only 9 minutes.) Press "cancel" to stop the keep-warm feature, then let sit for 10 minutes before releasing the pressure.

2. Drain off most of the excess liquid (save some!), then add the lime juice and salt; mix well, then serve as desired. Leftovers will keep in the fridge for up to 5 days.

Hands-on time:

2 MINUTES

Cook time:

22 MINUTES PLUS TIME TO
COME TO PRESSURE

Makes about 5 cups (860 g)

sweet and smoky black-eyed peas

2 cups (335 g) dried black-eyed peas

1 yellow onion, diced

2 teaspoons smoked paprika

½ teaspoon liquid smoke (optional)

1 teaspoon pink Himalayan salt, plus more to taste

1. Put the beans, onion, smoked paprika, and 6 cups (1.4 L) water in a pressure cooker. Close the Instant Pot, set the valve to sealing, and cook on Manual High pressure for 22 minutes. (If you soaked your beans, drain and rinse them, and then put them in the pressure cooker for only 5 minutes.) Press "cancel" to stop

the keep-warm feature, then let sit for 10 minutes before releasing the pressure.

2. Drain off most of the excess liquid (save some!), then add the liquid smoke (if using) and salt; mix well, taste for salt, then serve as desired. Leftovers will keep in the fridge for up to 5 days.

Hands-on time:

5 MINUTES

Cook time:

28 MINUTES PLUS TIME TO
COME TO PRESSURE

Makes about 5 cups (860 g)

rosemary garlic black beans

2 cups (390 g) dried black beans

1 sprig fresh rosemary, stem removed, leaves finely chopped

5 cloves garlic, thinly sliced

1 teaspoon pink Himalayan salt, plus more to taste

1. Put the beans, rosemary, garlic, and 6 cups (1.4 L) water in a pressure cooker. Close the Instant Pot, set the valve to sealing, and cook on Manual High pressure for 28 minutes. (If you soaked your beans, drain and rinse them, and then put them in the pressure cooker for only 8 minutes.) Press

"cancel" to stop the keep-warm feature, then let sit for 10 minutes before releasing the pressure.

2. Drain off most of the excess liquid (save some!), then add the salt; mix well, taste for salt, then serve as desired. Leftovers will keep in the fridge for up to 5 days.

cajun-spiced beans and rice

A lot of plant-based peeps seem to overlook (or underrate?) the classic combination of beans and rice. Sure, they taste a little bland on their own, but when you add some veggies and seasonings they transform into a hearty, flavorful, and budget-friendly dish that is just as tasty as it is versatile. Think Tex-Mex, Indian, Mediterranean, and even Asian!

This dish takes inspiration from the classic Creole version. Long-grain brown rice and cooked kidney beans combine with the Cajun "trinity" (onion, bell pepper, and celery) and some Cajun seasoning to make a filling main. You'll make everything in the Instant Pot—saving you time and extra dishwashing! This meal may not look the prettiest, but it tastes so freakin' good, so don't skip it. If you can't find salt-free Cajun seasoning, you can make your own blend—there are lots of recipes online.

½   yellow onion, diced

1   carrot, peeled and diced

1   green bell pepper, diced

3   ribs celery, chopped

3   tablespoons salt-free Cajun seasoning

1½   cups (295 g) uncooked long-grain brown rice

1½   cups (280 g) cooked red kidney beans

1   teaspoon pink Himalayan salt

Freshly ground black pepper

Hot sauce, for serving (optional)

1. Turn a pressure cooker on to the "sauté" setting and put ½ cup (120 ml) water, the onion, carrot, bell pepper, and celery in the pot. Sauté for 3 to 5 minutes, until the onion is translucent.

2. Add the Cajun seasoning and sauté for an additional minute, then add the rice, beans, salt, and 1½ cups (360 ml) water. Close the Instant Pot, set the valve to "sealing," then cook on Manual High pressure for 25 minutes.

3. Let the pot naturally release pressure for 10 minutes, then manually move the valve from "sealing" to "venting" to release the remaining pressure. Fluff the rice with a spatula, and season with black pepper and additional salt to taste, if necessary.

4. Serve warm; leftovers will keep in the fridge for up to 5 days.

note: If you soaked your beans, drain and rinse well. Cook on Manual high pressure for 9 minutes, then let sit for 10 minutes before releasing the pressure.

tex-mex black bean chili

Chili was one of my staple meals as a vegan in college. Not only are all of the ingredients super affordable, but it's also filling, cooks quickly, and keeps and reheats well for meal prep. My recipe would vary slightly every week based on what veggies were on sale at the grocery store, but I had a few staple recipes that I always went back to, this Tex-Mex chili being one of them.

I used canned beans in college, but now I prefer to cook my own dried beans using my pressure cooker. Even though canned beans are relatively cheap, dried legumes are even less expensive! Plus, a lot of canned beans (and vegetables, for that matter) are loaded with sodium and other preservatives. Soaking the black beans in advance helps to make this meal even faster—you really only need ten minutes in the pressure cooker to make them soft and tender. Finally, if you've never added salsa to your chili before, you're in for a treat. It adds this amazing depth of flavor that's almost impossible to create with its component ingredients.

FOR THE CHILI:

- ½   yellow onion, diced
- 3   cloves garlic, minced
- 3   jalapeños, seeded and diced
- ½   bunch fresh cilantro, finely chopped
- 1   tablespoon chili powder
- 1   tablespoon ground cumin
- 2   cups (390 g) dried black beans, soaked in water overnight
- 1   cup (240 ml) mild, medium, or hot store-bought salsa
- 1   (28-ounce/794 g) can petite diced tomatoes

OPTIONAL TOPPINGS:

- Cashew Cream (page 211)
- Nutritional yeast
- Fresh cilantro

1. Turn a pressure cooker on to the "sauté" setting; when it's warm, put the onion, garlic, and ¼ cup (60 ml) water in the pot and sauté until translucent, 3 to 5 minutes. Add the jalapeños, cilantro, chili powder, and cumin, then cook for another 1 to 2 minutes.

2. Press "cancel" to turn off the heat, then add the beans, salsa, tomatoes, and 2 cups (480 ml) water. Close the Instant Pot, set the valve to "sealing," and cook on Manual High pressure for 10 minutes.

3. When the timer goes off, press "cancel" to stop the keep-warm feature, then let the Instant Pot sit for 5 minutes before manually moving the valve from "sealing" to "venting" to release the remaining pressure. Uncover the pot and let the chili sit for 5 minutes to thicken.

4. Divide the chili among serving bowls, then top with cashew cream, nutritional yeast, and cilantro as desired. Leftovers will keep in the fridge for up to 5 days, or can be frozen for up to 2 months.

note: If you'd like to increase the heat in this chili, use a spicy salsa. You can also leave a few of the jalapeño seeds in for extra kick!

chickpea tikka masala

I actually grew up eating a fair amount of Indian food, at least when my family and I went out to eat. Indian food is naturally vegetarian friendly, so my family of five knew that there would be enough options on the menu for all of us to find something to enjoy.

I tend to use a lot of spices and flavor in my recipes, and I think part of this comes from my early exposure to (and love of) Indian food. While it actually has both British and Indian roots, tikka masala is a staple on most restaurant menus and a favorite of many. It's often made with animal protein, but today we're simmering fiber-rich chickpeas with our creamy, luscious, and well-spiced tomato sauce for a hearty, cozy, and comforting entrée. If you already have a tikka masala spice blend in your pantry, ditch the mix of dried spices and use 2½ tablespoons of that instead.

FOR THE CHICKPEA TIKKA MASALA:

- 1 large yellow onion
- 4 large cloves garlic
- 2 serrano peppers
- 1 (28-ounce/800 g) can diced fire-roasted tomatoes
- 1 (13½-ounce/400 ml) can full-fat coconut milk
- 2-inch (5 cm) piece of fresh ginger, peeled
- ½ bunch fresh cilantro
- 4 teaspoons garam masala
- 1 teaspoon ground turmeric
- 1½ teaspoons ground cumin
- 1 teaspoon chile powder
- 1 teaspoon pink Himalayan salt
- 5 cups (860 g) cooked salt-free chickpeas (about 3 cans)

FOR SERVING:

Cooked brown rice

Finely chopped fresh cilantro

1. Finely dice half of the onion, finely chop the garlic, and seed and finely chop the serrano peppers; set aside.

2. Add the other half of the onion to a high-speed blender with the tomatoes, coconut milk, ginger, cilantro, spices, and salt. Blend for 30 seconds, or until a smooth sauce forms.

3. Turn a pressure cooker on to the "sauté" setting and add the diced onion, garlic, serrano peppers, and ¼ cup (60 ml) water to the pot. Sauté until translucent, 3 to 5 minutes.

4. Press "cancel" to turn the pot off, then stir in the chickpeas and blended sauce. Close the lid on the Instant Pot, set the pressure valve to "sealing," then cook on Manual High pressure for 6 minutes. Press "cancel" to turn off the keep-warm function, then let the pot naturally release pressure for 5 minutes before manually moving the valve from "sealing" to "venting."

5. Uncover, mix, and let sit for 5 minutes before serving with rice and cilantro. Refrigerate leftovers in an airtight container for up to 1 week.

easy lentil bolognese

Traditional bolognese is made with ground meat, but I swap that for heart-healthy lentils, which not only have 7–12 grams of protein per ½ cooked cup, but are also a great source of iron and dietary fiber. While lentils are an excellent protein substitute for meat, they are missing a little something in both the texture and flavor departments. The addition of finely chopped mushrooms and walnuts help to give this sauce that deep umami flavor we're looking for, as well as a good dose of healthy fats. You can skip the wine if you prefer not to cook with it, but it does add an extra layer of flavor that really helps to make the dish. Plus, you can enjoy a glass while you cook ;)

This recipe makes a large batch of sauce, which makes it great for meal prep. You can enjoy your leftovers throughout the week, or freeze half of it for later. I prefer to cook my pasta day-of while I reheat my leftovers, as it doesn't take long to cook and always dries out in the fridge when prepped in advance.

---

2 ribs celery

2 carrots, peeled

½ yellow onion

2 cups (480 ml) vegetable broth

8 ounces (225 g) cremini mushrooms

½ cup (120 ml) dry white wine

½ cup (55 g) walnuts

½ bunch fresh parsley, large stems removed

6 to 7 large fresh basil leaves

1 (6-ounce/170 g) can tomato paste

1 cup (195 g) dried brown lentils

1 (28-ounce/794 g) can diced fire-roasted tomatoes

Salt and freshly ground black pepper

16 ounces (455 g) gluten-free spaghetti

1. Roughly chop the celery, carrots, and onion into equal-size pieces, then put them in a food processor and pulse until finely chopped. Turn a pressure cooker on to the "sauté" setting; when it's warm, add the chopped vegetables and ½ cup (120 ml) of the broth. Cook until the onions are translucent, 3 to 5 minutes.

2. In the meantime, pulse the mushrooms in the food processor until finely chopped. Add them to the Instant Pot, along with the wine, and sauté for an additional 3 minutes while you pulse the walnuts, basil, and parsley together in the food processor. Add the nut and herb mixture to the pot and cook for an additional minute.

3. Stir the tomato paste into the sautéed vegetables; when it's evenly distributed, add the lentils, the remaining broth, and tomatoes and mix well. Press the "cancel" setting to turn off the pot, then cover the pot, set the valve to "sealing," and cook the sauce on Manual High pressure for 15 minutes. While the sauce is cooking, prepare your gluten-free pasta according to the package instructions.

4. Manually release the pressure when the timer goes off, then uncover the pot and stir the sauce. Let the sauce

sit uncovered for 5 minutes to thicken, then season with salt and pepper to taste, if necessary. Serve over cooked pasta, or as desired. Leftovers will keep in the fridge for up to 5 days, or in the freezer for up to 2 months.

note: Did you know that some wine isn't vegan? Unfortunately, some companies use fish bladders in the filtering process. Some producers will note if they are vegan on the bottle, but Barnivore. com is also a great resource for determining whether any alcohol you consume is cruelty-free.

Hands-on time:
10 MINUTES

Cook time:
5 MINUTES PLUS TIME TO
COME TO PRESSURE

Serves 2 or 3

instant pot pumpkin pasta

The first few months I had my pressure cooker I mostly stuck to batch cooking rice and beans—to be honest, I was a little intimidated by it! Then one day I was scrolling through my Instagram feed and saw that one of my friends had cooked pasta . . . in their Instant Pot?! My world was forever changed, and I knew I needed to venture outside my comfort zone ASAP.

Instant Pot pasta is kind of, well, magical. Cooking the pasta in just the right amount of liquid creates both perfectly cooked noodles *and* a creamy, starch-based sauce without the need for any added oils or plant-based fats. You can fold up to ½ cup (120 ml) Cashew Cream (page 211) into the cooked dish for some extra richness, but I think it's just as satisfying without it. In terms of pasta, try to stick to a rice or quinoa and corn–based variety; legume-based pasta tends to fall apart in the pressure cooker. If you'd like to make this meal heartier or add some textural variety, fold in a couple of handfuls of baby spinach or top with some roasted veggies, like Maple-Glazed Brussels Sprouts (page 127).

---

2   cups (480 ml) low-sodium vegetable broth

½   cup (120 g) pumpkin puree

⅓   cup (25 g) nutritional yeast

½   teaspoon paprika

½   teaspoon garlic powder

¼   teaspoon grated nutmeg

3   fresh sage leaves, crushed

8   ounces (225 g) gluten-free pasta

Salt and freshly ground black pepper

1. Put the broth, pumpkin, nutritional yeast, paprika, garlic powder, nutmeg, and sage in a pressure cooker; mix until a smooth, slightly thick liquid forms. Add the pasta to the pot, then close the pressure cooker and set the valve to "sealing."

2. Cook the pasta on Manual High pressure for 5 minutes, then immediately release the pressure by moving the valve from "sealing" to "venting." Press the "cancel" button to turn off the keep-warm feature and prevent the pasta from overcooking.

3. Stir the pasta well and add salt and pepper to taste, if necessary. Let the pasta sit for 5 minutes in the Instant Pot before stirring again and spooning into serving bowls—this allows the sauce to thicken.

note: Crushing the sage leaves breaks down their cell walls and allows more flavor to escape into the pasta, without having to bite on bits of this tougher herb throughout your meal. I suggest placing your sage on a cutting board and pounding it out with the base of a heavy drinking glass. The leaves will turn darker in color when they've been successfully crushed.

dill-icious mashed potatoes

Are there people out there who don't like mashed potatoes? I feel like anyone who says that is just lying to themself and maaaaaay just be slightly afraid of carbs. Sure, most classic mashed potato recipes are loaded with butter and cream. These (obviously) are not, but are still just as comforting and delightful. Also, did you know that cooked white potatoes have been scientifically recognized as one of the most satiating foods? Don't fear the white potato, people! Embrace it. Especially when it's mashed into a creamy goodness and seasoned with heaps of garlic and fresh herbs.

Not sure how to serve these mashed potatoes? Sometimes I just top them with peas, chickpeas, and a good drizzle of Miso Tahini Gravy (page 216) and call it a day—kind of like a deconstructed shepherd's pie. If you're not a fan of eating them like a main course, I guess I understand. They're also just as yummy alongside homemade veggie burgers, plant-based sausages, or some Sweet and Smoky Tempeh (see page 54).

1½ pounds (680 g) gold or red potatoes, cut into 1-inch (2.5 cm) pieces

2 cloves garlic, minced

1 tablespoon distilled white vinegar

½ teaspoon pink Himalayan salt, plus more to taste

1 tablespoon nutritional yeast

⅓ cup (80 ml) Cashew Cream (page 211)

1 tablespoon chopped fresh dill

2 tablespoons chopped fresh chives

Salt and freshly ground black pepper

1. Put the potatoes, garlic, vinegar, and salt in a pressure cooker. Cover the potatoes with water—3 to 4 cups (700 to 950 ml), then close the pressure cooker and set the valve to "sealing." Cook on Manual High pressure for 8 minutes.

2. Turn off the pressure cooker and manually release the pressure by moving the valve from "sealing" to "venting." Cover the valve with a dish towel to avoid steam and splatter! Drain the potatoes and return them to the Instant Pot, but save the cooking liquid.

3. Add the cashew cream, nutritional yeast, and ¼ cup (60 ml) of the cooking liquid to the pot with the potatoes. Use a potato masher to mash the potatoes until you're satisfied with the texture—I like mine to be a little chunky. If the mixture is too thick, add additional cooking liquid as desired. Add the dill and chives to the potatoes and fold them into the mixture; season with salt and pepper to taste, then serve warm.

note: Peeling the potatoes is totally optional, as long as you rinse them well. I like to leave the peels on for some extra texture in my spuds!

8 | super-quick fixes

Good news—you don't have to eat boring beans and rice or sad, sad leftovers on those nights when you're short on time. All of the following meals are quick, easy, and, most importantly, tasty. So the next time you're pondering takeout (again), stop for a second and browse through this chapter. You'll have a nutritious *and* delicious dinner on your table in thirty-five minutes or less—and that's a promise.

vegan pad thai

buffalo cauliflower penne

Salty meets spicy meets creamy in this classic vegan-restaurant-option-turned-main-dish. Okay, woah, that's a lot of hyphens. What you really need to know, though, is that this dish is foolproof and delish! It's kind of like we took the Golden Cauliflower Wings (page 132), stripped the sauce (but kept the crispy), and chucked it on some pasta. That sounds kind of odd, but this? This tastes absolutely amazing.

If you're looking for a macronutrient-complete meal, choose a bean-based pasta for a healthy dose of complex carbs and plant-based protein.

Pink Himalayan salt

2½ cups (370 g) cauliflower florets; about ½ head

2 teaspoons plus ¼ cup (20 g) nutritional yeast

½ teaspoon smoked paprika

8 ounces (225 g) gluten-free penne (or pasta of choice)

½ cup (120 ml) Cashew Cream (page 211)

⅓ cup (75 ml) Buffalo hot sauce

½ teaspoon garlic powder

½ teaspoon onion powder

Chopped fresh parsley

1. Preheat the oven to 450°F (230°C) and line a baking sheet with parchment paper or a silicone mat. Bring a large pot of salted water to a boil.

2. Put the cauliflower in a medium bowl and toss with the 2 teaspoons nutritional yeast, the smoked paprika, and ¼ teaspoon salt. Spread evenly across the baking sheet, then bake on the top rack of the oven for 15 to 18 minutes.

3. When the water is boiling, add the pasta and cook according to the package instructions. Drain the pasta, but do not rinse. Whisk the remaining nutritional yeast, cashew cream, Buffalo sauce, garlic powder, and onion powder together in the pot, then return the pasta to the pot and mix well.

4. Divide the pasta evenly among serving bowls, then top with the cauliflower and parsley. Serve warm; leftovers will keep in the fridge for up to 3 days.

one-pot mushroom stroganoff

My mom didn't cook anything overly extravagant for our family, but everything she did cook was (1) really dang cozy, and (2) really dang delicious. I always looked forward to the cooler months when we'd have creamy soups and crusty bread for dinner—she would always throw an extra lone veggie or two into the soup broth so I could look for a "surprise" as I emptied my bowl. Sometimes she'd make a vegetarian version of beef stroganoff, too. We didn't have it often, but those bouncy noodles and that umami-loaded sauce always stuck with me.

There's a reason this recipe is one of the most popular recipes on my blog, and why I also chose to include it in this book. It's easy, fast, and satisfying to the point where it's almost mind-blowing that this chunky, creamy, and flavor-loaded dish is made entirely from plants. Seriously, friends: Whether you serve this to a die-hard vegan, a picky eater, or a carnivore, they're gonna love it. Gluten-free rotini mimics the classic egg noodle in most stroganoffs, though you could swap it out for any other shorter noodle shape, like macaroni, bow ties, or penne. If you have a nut allergy, replace the cashew butter with canned coconut cream.

1	small yellow onion
10	ounces (280 g) cremini mushrooms
4	cups gluten-free rotini, or pasta of choice
4	cups (960 ml) vegetable broth (see Note)
2	tablespoons nutritional yeast
¼	teaspoon freshly ground black pepper, plus more to taste
⅓	cup (90 g) cashew butter
1	tablespoon fresh lemon juice
	Salt
	Chopped fresh parsley

1. Peel the onion, cut it in half, and then thinly slice it into half "rings." Clean the mushrooms using a damp paper towel or cloth, then cut them in half or quarters, depending on their size. You want to keep the mushrooms relatively large, as they will shrink when cooking and are meant to imitate beef in this recipe.

2. Heat a large pot over medium heat; when it's warm, add ¼ cup (60 ml) water and the onion; cook until the onion is translucent, 3 to 5 minutes.

3. Add the mushrooms, pasta, broth, nutritional yeast, and pepper, stirring well. Bring to a boil over high heat, then reduce the heat to medium and simmer for 10 to 15 minutes, stirring occasionally to ensure nothing sticks to the bottom of the pan.

4. Remove from the heat, then stir in the cashew butter and

lemon juice. Taste the pasta and add salt and pepper to taste, if necessary. Transfer to serving bowls and top with parsley. Serve warm; leftovers will keep in the fridge for up to 5 days.

note: If you can get your hands on a vegan beef-flavored bouillon, use that instead of vegetable broth—some grocery stores carry it, and you can also purchase it online. This stroganoff will taste delicious either way, but the beefy flavor helps to make this plant-based recipe even more satisfying and realistic.

kale pesto pasta

Remember that kale pesto we slathered on avocado toast (page 23)? Now it's time to serve it up with some pasta. This dish is perfect for a busy weeknight because it's fast, easy, and oh so satisfying. Prepare the pesto while the pasta cooks, and if you'd like to garnish your pasta with additional nuts, add a few extra to the pan and toast them along with the pesto ingredients.

Drain your pasta, but don't rinse it—this will help the pesto stick to the noodles better. I like to use a bean-based pasta for an extra boost of plant protein, but a pasta with a brown rice, corn, or quinoa base will also work well here. Opt for spiral shapes or pasta with ridges over straight noodles if you really want to get a good, saucy coat on there.

This dish can be served either hot or cold, making it a perfect year-round weekday lunch or picnic side. If you're prepping it in advance, toss the noodles with the pesto before storing in the fridge to prevent them from drying out. Adding some fresh tomatoes and/or roasted veggies will make this an even heartier plant-packed meal.

Salt

16 ounces gluten-free pasta

1 batch of Kale Pesto (page 219)

Freshly ground black pepper

Toasted pine nuts and macadamia nuts

Fresh basil

1. Bring a large pot of salted water to a boil and cook your pasta according to the package instructions.

2. Drain your pasta, but do not rinse it. Return the pasta to the pot and use a spatula to fold the pesto into the pasta until all pieces are evenly coated. Add salt and pepper to taste, if necessary.

3. Portion the pasta among serving plates, then top with nuts and basil. Serve warm; leftovers will keep in the fridge for up to 5 days.

one-pot quinoa with spring vegetables

This dish features protein-packed quinoa, creamy white beans, and lots of spring veggies—it's not just a one-pot recipe, but a one-dish meal. Toasting the quinoa before adding the remaining ingredients helps to remove some of its bitterness and replace it with a well-rounded, nutty flavor. Tossing the cooked quinoa with some crunchy, bright, and fresh spring vegetables adds even more flavor and color, making this easy meal a crowd-pleaser that can be served either warm or chilled.

It's great on its own, but a drizzle of Everyday Tahini Sauce (page 212), Jalapeño Ranch (page 232), or Rosemary Tahini Sauce (page 212) wouldn't hurt. Some diced avocado, would be a nice addition to your plate, too, if you happen to have a ripe one on your countertop.

1⅓ cups (150 g) uncooked quinoa

2⅔ cups (630 ml) low-sodium vegetable broth

2 (15-ounce/425 g) cans cannellini beans, drained and rinsed

2 carrots, peeled and finely diced

2 green onions, sliced; keep white and green portions seperate

1 cup (105 g) sugar snap peas, cut in half

4 radishes, thinly sliced

¼ bunch fresh parsley, stems removed, leaves chopped

Salt and freshly ground black pepper

1. Heat a large nonstick pot over medium-high heat and add the dry quinoa to it. Toast the quinoa for 2 to 3 minutes, stirring occasionally. Raise the heat to high and add the broth, beans, carrots, and the white portion of the green onions. Stir well; when the mixture comes to a boil, cover, reduce the heat to low, and cook for 15 minutes. Remove from the heat and let the pot sit, covered, for an additional 5 minutes before fluffing the quinoa with a fork.

2. Transfer the quinoa to a serving bowl and fold in the sugar snap peas, radishes, green portions of the green onions, and parsley. Season with salt and pepper to taste, if necessary. Serve warm or chilled.

giant green bowls

Do you ever have those days when you feel like you just need to eat a giant, giant salad? I know I sure do, and when I have that craving, I almost always make these Giant Green Bowls. They are packed— and I mean packed—with *allll* the good stuff, like kale, greens, edamame, and avocado. But don't worry, my salad-hating friends: These bowls are also drenched in a creamy, nut-free Jalapeño Ranch (page 232), which makes eating an enormous bowl of green stuff actually kind of enjoyable!

This recipe is inspired by one of my favorite dishes from Blossoming Lotus, a vegan restaurant here in Portland, Oregon. I almost never order steamed veggies when I go out to eat (I mean, c'mon—I can totally do that at home), but dang, do they know how to do it right. Sometimes I'll make a batch of crispy tofu from the Sheet Pan Teriyaki Bowls (page 171) sans teriyaki sauce and totally deck these out. Fair warning: This recipe makes a lot of food, so come with an appetite.

⅔ cup (110 g) uncooked tricolor quinoa

8 ounces (225 g) fresh or frozen (thawed) shelled edamame

1 bunch curly kale, stems removed, chopped

1 ounce salad mix

½ regular cucumber, peeled and sliced

1 avocado, sliced

Jalapeño Ranch (page 232)

Hemp hearts

Nutritional yeast

1. Put the quinoa in a medium pot with 1⅓ cups (320 ml) water and cook according to the package instructions.

2. In the meantime, fill a large pot with a steamer basket with 2 inches (5 cm) water; cover and bring to a boil over high heat. Reduce the heat to medium-low, add the edamame, re-cover, and steam for 5 minutes. Add the kale to the basket and steam for an additional 2 minutes, or until tender.

3. Assemble the bowls by filling them with salad mix, quinoa, steamed kale, and edamame. Top with cucumber, avocado, dressing, and a sprinkle of hemp hearts and nutritional yeast.

note: If you don't have a pot with a steamer basket you can use a fine-mesh metal strainer instead!

pineapple unfried rice

The best thing to do with leftover rice? Make fried rice, of course! This thirty-minute recipe adds sweet and juicy pineapple to this classic grain-based dish for a fun, refreshing twist. You can use either brown or white rice for this recipe, but it is best to use leftover rice instead of freshly cooked. Refrigerating the rice slightly dries it out, which allows it to better absorb all the yummy flavors we'll be cooking it with.

Traditional fried rice is, well, fried, but today we're skipping that step! Cooking the rice with pineapple helps to give it a glossy and caramelized coating, without the use of any added oil. If you cook the rice long enough and let the nonstick pan get dry, you'll be able to get some crispy rice bits in the final product, too. Just be sure to use a sturdy wooden or plastic spatula so you can scoop all that goodness into your bowl, or pineapple bowl if you want to go the extra mile!

---

2   cloves garlic, minced

2   large green onions, sliced; keep white and green portions separate

1   large carrot, peeled and shredded

2   cups (8 ounces) sugar snap peas, cut in half

1   cup (175 g) finely diced fresh pineapple

3   cups (410 g) cooked brown or white rice

3   tablespoons tamari

    Sesame seeds, for ganish

1. Heat a large nonstick skillet over medium-low heat and add ¼ cup (60 ml) water. When the water starts to steam, add the garlic and the white portions of the green onions and sauté for 60 seconds, until the onions are translucent. Add the carrot, sugar snap peas, and pineapple to the pan and sauté for an additional 2 to 3 minutes.

2. Add the rice and tamari; mix well. Sauté for 5 to 6 minutes, until no moisture is at the bottom of the pan and the rice looks sticky and glossy.

3. Transfer to serving bowls and top with sesame seeds and the green portions of the green onions; serve warm.

Hands-on time:
15 MINUTES

Cook time:
20 MINUTES

Serves 2 as-is
or 4 with rice

garlicky green bean stir-fry with sticky orange tempeh

Say goodbye to greasy takeout food, and hello to this bright, fresh, and veggie-packed alternative! A garlicky green bean and mushroom stir-fry serves as a nutritious base for our sticky orange tempeh, which is actually just as wholesome, thanks to the Healthy Orange Sauce.

If you'd like to make this meal even heartier, serve it with some cooked brown or white rice. And don't forget the extra orange sauce to drizzle on top!

FOR THE STICKY ORANGE TEMPEH:

- 1 cup (240 ml) vegetable broth
- ½ cup (120 ml) Healthy Orange Sauce (page 227)
- 1 (8-ounce/227 g) package tempeh, cut into ½-inch (12 mm) strips

FOR THE GARLICKY GREEN BEANS:

- ¼ yellow onion, cut into thin strips
- 5 ounces (140 g) cremini mushrooms, sliced
- 2 cloves garlic, minced
- 4 cups (370 g) trimmed and halved green beans
- 1 tablespoon low-sodium tamari
- ¼ teaspoon red chile flakes (optional)
- ¼ cup (60 ml) Healthy Orange Sauce (page 227)

1. Make the sticky orange tempeh: Whisk the broth and orange sauce together in the base of a deep sauté pan or large pot. Add the tempeh and place over high heat.

2. When the mixture starts to bubble, reduce the heat to medium-high and use a spatula to flip the tempeh every 2 to 3 minutes to ensure both sides cook evenly.

3. The tempeh will start to sizzle when most of the water has evaporated, after 8 to 10 minutes. At this point, begin to rapidly flip the tempeh to caramelize each side and coat it in the remainder of the sauce. Sauté for an additional 2 to 3 minutes, then remove from the heat and let the tempeh sit in the pan while you finish the green beans.

4. While the tempeh is cooking, heat a large nonstick sauté pan over medium heat; when it's warm, add 2 tablespoons water, the onion, mushrooms, garlic, green beans, tamari, and chile flakes. Sauté for 7 to 10 minutes, until the onion is translucent and the green beans are cooked to your liking.

5. Reduce the heat to low and stir the orange sauce into the mixture to heat through. When it's warm, transfer the veggies to serving plates and top with the tempeh. Serve warm.

vegan pad thai

There's a reason this sweet, salty, and spicy noodle dish is so popular—it's really freakin' delicious! Here we'll swap the scrambled eggs for scrambled tofu, and load our noodles up with veggies for a heartier meal. A lot of restaurants use fish sauce in their pad Thai, but that's easy to leave out without sacrificing flavor.

Brown rice noodles add some extra undetectable fiber to this dish, but you can use white rice noodles if you prefer. Feel free to omit the peanuts if you have an allergy. You can also adjust the spice level of this dish via the amount of sriracha—I like my noodles spicy, so sometimes I add a little extra.

- 8 ounces (225 g) brown rice noodles
- 8 ounces (225 g) extra-firm tofu, drained (½ block)
- ¼ teaspoon ground turmeric
- ¼ teaspoon pink Himalayan salt or *kala namak* (black salt; see page 42)
- 4 cloves garlic, minced
- 2 green onions, sliced; keep white and green portions separate
- 1 red bell pepper, sliced
- 1 large carrot, peeled and cut into matchsticks
- ⅔ cup (165 ml) vegetable broth
- 3 tablespoons coconut sugar
- 2 tablespoons low-sodium tamari
- 1 to 3 tablespoons sriracha, based on heat preference
- 1 tablespoon arrowroot powder or cornstarch
- 1 cup (105 g) mung bean sprouts
- Juice of ½ lime, plus lime wedges for serving
- ¼ bunch fresh cilantro, chopped
- ⅓ cup (50 g) dry-roasted peanuts

1. Bring a medium pot of water to a boil and cook the noodles according to the package instructions; drain, rinse, and set aside.

2. In the meantime, heat a large nonstick pan over medium heat with ¼ cup (60 ml) water. Use your hands to crumble the tofu into the pan, then add the turmeric and stir well. Cook for 3 to 5 minutes, then transfer to a small bowl and stir in the salt; set aside.

3. Add an additional ¼ cup (60 ml) water to the same pan, along with the garlic and white portions of the green onions. Sauté for 3 minutes, until translucent. Add the bell pepper and carrot to the pan and sauté until tender, 3 to 5 minutes.

4. While the vegetables are cooking, whisk the broth, coconut sugar, tamari, sriracha, and arrowroot powder together in a small bowl until smooth and thick. Add the mixture to the pan of sautéing vegetables and simmer for 3 minutes, until the sauce begins to thicken.

5. Add the noodles, tofu, bean sprouts, the green portions of the green onions, and lime juice to the pan; stir until everything is evenly combined and warm. Divide the pad Thai evenly between serving plates and top with cilantro, peanuts, and lime wedges. Serve warm.

9 | marvelous mains

Burgers, bowls, and rice bakes—oh my! These recipes are for nights when you have a little more time to put some love into your meal. They might have longer bake times or a few more steps, but don't worry: Every single one of these recipes is so dang worth it. And if you're still a little dubious, grab a friend and cook together! Laughter and drinks are optional, but highly recommended.

crispy veggie flatbreads,
two ways

sheet pan teriyaki bowls

Fluffy white rice, crispy roasted broccoli, and sticky teriyaki tofu combine to make a cozy and super-satisfying meal. And the best part? You only need one bowl, a baking sheet, and a small pot to make it. Roasting the broccoli on the same pan as the tofu reduces both hands-on kitchen time and cleanup, giving you more time to live your life . . . or maybe make dessert?

While this recipe has a long-ish cook time, the steps and cleanup are incredibly easy. Leftovers will last in the fridge for up to five days and can be reheated in a pinch, making it a great recipe for meal prep. The crispy teriyaki tofu is a slightly modified version of the famous crispy tofu recipe on my blog. To make the plain crispy tofu for an incredibly easy add-on to practically any of your favorite recipes, simply leave out the teriyaki sauce and bake it for 25 minutes after you flip it.

FOR THE CRISPY TERIYAKI TOFU:

1 (14-ounce/397 g) block extra-firm tofu, drained and pressed

1 tablespoon low-sodium tamari

2 tablespoons nutritional yeast

¼ cup (60 ml) Date-Sweetened Teriyaki Sauce (page 228)

FOR THE TERIYAKI BOWLS:

1 head of broccoli

1 cup (225 g) white jasmine rice

Date-Sweetened Teriyaki Sauce (page 228), to drizzle on top

1 green onion, thinly sliced

1 tablespoon toasted sesame seeds

note: Add some extra veggies in with the broccoli if you're looking for more variety!

1. Make the crispy teriyaki tofu: Preheat the oven to 425°F (220°C) and line a baking sheet with a silicone mat or parchment paper. Cut the block of tofu in half lengthwise, then cut each half block into 16 even cubes.

2. Put the tofu in a large bowl, drizzle the tamari over it, then use a spatula to gently toss until evenly coated. Sprinkle the nutritional yeast over the tofu, then mix again. Transfer the cubes to the baking sheet, leaving an equal amount of space between the cubes. Bake on the top rack of the oven for 20 minutes.

3. In the meantime, make the teriyaki sauce, cut the broccoli into bite-sized florets, and cook the rice according to the package instructions. After the tofu has baked for 20 minutes, flip the tofu with a spatula and move it over to one side of the baking sheet; spread the broccoli florets on the other side, then return to the top rack of the oven and bake for 15 minutes.

4. Remove the baking sheet from the oven; place the tofu in the same mixing bowl as before, and toss it with the ¼ cup (60 ml) teriyaki sauce. Return the saucy tofu to the baking sheet and bake on the top rack of the oven for a final 5 minutes.

5. Divide the cooked rice among serving bowls, then top with roasted broccoli, crispy tofu, and an extra drizzle of sauce. Garnish with green onion and sesame seeds, then serve warm.

taco mac and cheese

Tacos are great and all, but have you ever had Taco Mac and Cheese? This, my friends, is a total game changer. This comforting combination of two of my favorite food groups is creamy, spicy, and so. dang. satisfying. And while it may taste decadent, it's still made from whole-food ingredients and is completely oil-free. Which means you can sit back, relax, and thoroughly enjoy a bowl without a total crash and heavy food coma thirty minutes later.

I've made this nacho cheese–inspired sauce using both cashews and tahini, and enjoy both equally. The cashews provide a neutral, subtly sweet flavor, while the tahini provides a bit of a nutty tang, similar to a cheddar-style cheese. If you do opt for the tahini, add it to the blender with the plant milk, jalapeños, and spices instead of boiling it with the potatoes and carrots. Finally, a lot of store-brand chili powders are simply a mix of chili-style spices and salt; try to find pure ancho chile powder for maximum flavor.

FOR THE SAUCE:

- 1 cup (160 g) peeled and diced russet potato (½-inch/12 mm cubes; about 1 medium)
- ½ cup (80 g) peeled and diced carrot (½-inch/12 mm cubes; 1 medium)
- ¼ cup (35 g) raw cashews, or 2 tablespoons tahini
- ½ cup (120 ml) nondairy milk
- 3 tablespoons nutritional yeast
- 2 tablespoons pickled jalapeños, chopped
- 1 tablespoon pickled jalapeño brine
- ½ teaspoon garlic powder
- ¾ teaspoon pink Himalayan salt, plus more to taste

FOR THE TACO "MEAT":

- 2 cups (340 g) cooked brown lentils
- ½ cup (45 g) raw sunflower seeds
- 1 teaspoon ancho chile powder
- 1 teaspoon onion powder
- ½ teaspoon ground cumin
- ¼ teaspoon cayenne pepper
- ½ teaspoon dried oregano

  Salt and freshly ground black pepper

FOR SERVING:

- 8 ounces (225 g) gluten-free macaroni, cooked according to package instructions
- ¼ cup (25 g) finely shredded green cabbage
- 1 Roma tomato, diced
- 1 green onion, sliced

1. Make the sauce: Put the potatoes, carrots, and cashews in a medium pot. Cover with water and bring to a boil over high heat, then reduce the heat to medium-low and simmer until the carrots are fork-tender, 8 to 10 minutes.

2. Drain the potato mixture in a colander, then immediately refill the pot with water, cover, and bring to a boil over high heat. Add the macaroni to the pot and cook according to the package directions. Drain the macaroni, but do not rinse.

3. While the macaroni is cooking, put the drained vegetables and cashews in a high-speed blender, along

with the milk, nutritional yeast, jalapeños, brine, garlic powder, and salt. Blend until smooth, 30 to 40 seconds.

4. While the macaroni cooks, prepare the taco "meat": Put the lentils, sunflower seeds, chile powder, onion powder, cumin, cayenne, oregano, and ½ cup (120 ml) water in a medium saucepan. Bring to a simmer over medium-high heat and

cook until all of the water has evaporated, 8 to 10 minutes. Season with salt and black pepper to taste.

5. Return the macaroni to the cooking pot over low heat and fold in the sauce. Transfer to serving bowls, then top with shredded cabbage, taco "meat," tomatoes, and green onion. Serve warm.

note: Use the thinnest setting on your mandoline to shred the cabbage; otherwise it will be tough to chew.

chipotle jackfruit enchiladas

My first-ever job (besides babysitting) was as a hostess in a Tex-Mex chain restaurant. While I couldn't eat most of the meat- and cheese-heavy menu, I thoroughly enjoyed my shift meals of beans, rice, and veggie enchiladas. I didn't grow up eating very much Tex-Mex food, so those saucy stuffed tortillas were a nice change of pace from my standard dinners of veggies, greens, and some sort of mock meat. These smoky jackfruit enchiladas are a tribute to those salsa-stained, chip crumb–dusted, fun-filled memories of early employment.

Ripe jackfruit has a distinct fruity taste, but green jackfruit does not—which makes it a great substitute for shredded meat. Just make sure you purchase canned jackfruit in brine, not syrup! The latter is the sugar-filled fruity stuff, and won't work in this recipe. Nowadays jackfruit in brine is available in many grocery stores, but you can also purchase it in larger quantities online. Also, did you know that cilantro stems have just as much flavor as their leaves? When finely diced, they practically melt into the smoky jackfruit filling—adding a ton of flavor without any weird stringy texture.

- 2 (14-ounce/400 g) cans jackfruit in brine (not syrup)
- ½ yellow onion, thinly sliced
- 6 ounces (170 g) cremini mushrooms, sliced
- 3 cloves garlic, minced
- ½ bunch fresh cilantro, finely chopped; keep stems and leaves separate
- 2 cups (475 ml) Chipotle Enchilada Sauce (page 231)
- 2 tablespoons plus ¼ cup (60 ml) Cashew Cream (page 211)
- 16 medium white corn tortillas, or tortillas of choice

  Diced avocado

1. Preheat the oven to 350°F (175°C).

2. Drain and rinse the jackfruit, then use your hands to break the pieces apart into shreds. Remove the jackfruit seeds and tough cores; discard the seeds, but roughly chop the jackfruit cores into small pieces and return to the shredded mixture. Set aside.

3. Heat a large nonstick pan over medium heat and add the onion, mushrooms, and garlic with ½ cup (120 ml) water. Sauté until the onions are translucent, 3 to 5 minutes. Add the jackfruit, the cilantro stems, ¾ cup (180 ml) of the enchilada sauce, and an additional ½ cup (120 ml) water. Simmer over medium heat for 5 to 7 minutes, stirring occasionally.

4. Whisk the remaining enchilada sauce with the 2 tablespoons cashew cream together in a small bowl. Use a spatula to spread ¼ cup (60 ml) of the creamy sauce in the base of a 3-quart (2.8-L) baking dish. Place 4 tortillas on a small plate

between two damp paper towels and microwave for 30 seconds. Fill each warmed tortilla with ⅓ cup of the jackfruit mixture, then roll it up and place them edge-side down in the baking dish. Repeat with the remaining tortillas and filling, microwaving in batches of four.

5. Top the enchiladas with the remaining enchilada sauce, then drizzle with the remaining cashew cream. Bake on the middle rack of the oven for 30 minutes. Top with the cilantro leaves and avocado, then serve warm. Leftovers will keep in the fridge for up to 5 days.

note: To reduce the day-of cook time, both the chipotle enchilada sauce and smoky jackfruit filling can be prepared and refrigerated up to 2 days in advance.

chunky portobello stew with chickpea dumplings

This stew screams cozy, and is pretty much a hug in a bowl. It's reminiscent of a pot roast or beef stew, with large chunks of carrots, celery, and portobello mushrooms. Do yourself a favor and put on your favorite sweater right before you enjoy it—or better yet, make yourself a cute little fire and snuggle up on the couch.

If you've never made drop dumplings before, you're in for a treat! These gluten-free dumplings are fluffy and slightly chewy, thanks to a combination of chickpea flour and oat flour. The trick is to mix the wet ingredients with the dry just before spooning the batter over the stew. Also, there is absolutely no peeking allowed after you put the lid on the pot! The dumplings need to be fully trapped in there for 15 minutes in order to absorb all of that yummy soup flavor and get nice and fluffy. If you're one of those curious people who just can't resist, use a pot with a glass lid so you can still get a glimpse of the action.

FOR THE PORTOBELLO STEW:

- 4 cups (950 ml) vegetable broth
- ½ yellow onion, diced
- 2 ribs celery, chopped
- 3 carrots, peeled and chopped
- ½ teaspoon smoked paprika
- ¼ teaspoon freshly ground black pepper, plus more to taste
- 8 ounces (225 g) portobello mushrooms, stems removed, cut into large chunks
- 1 pound (455 g) assorted mini potatoes, cut in half

FOR THE DROP DUMPLINGS:

- ½ cup plus 2 tablespoons (70 g) chickpea flour (garbanzo flour)
- ¼ cup (15 g) quick-cooking oats, blended to make oat flour
- 1 tablespoon nutritional yeast
- ¼ teaspoon baking powder
- ¼ teaspoon baking soda
- ¼ teaspoon pink Himalayan salt
- 6 tablespoons (90 ml) nondairy milk
- 1 teaspoon apple cider vinegar
- 2 tablespoons chopped fresh parsley, plus more for serving

1. Make the portobello stew: Put ¼ cup (60 ml) of the broth in a large nonstick pot over medium-high heat; when it's warm, add the onion and celery and sauté until translucent, 3 to 5 minutes. Add the carrots, smoked paprika, and pepper. Sauté for 2 minutes, then add the mushrooms, potatoes, and remaining vegetable broth. Stir well.

2. Bring the mixture to a boil over high heat, then cover and reduce the heat to medium-low; simmer for 10 minutes.

3. In the meantime, make the drop dumplings: Put the chickpea flour, oat flour, nutritional yeast, baking powder, baking soda, and salt in a medium bowl and whisk well. Add the milk and vinegar and gently stir until no lumps remain. Fold the parsley into the batter until just combined.

4. Remove the lid from the stew pot and carefully use a spoon to drop 2-tablespoon-size dollops of dumpling batter over the stew, until all of the batter has been used. Re-cover the stew and simmer for an additional 15 minutes; do not remove the lid from the pot during this time.

5. Uncover the pot, then ladle the stew and dumplings into serving bowls. Top with fresh parsley and extra pepper, if desired. Serve warm.

mediterranean rice bake

Did you know that you can make fluffy, perfectly cooked rice in your oven? Often referred to as the "dump and bake" casserole, this combination of rice, beans, seasonings, and just the right amount of vegetable broth has saved me from eating takeout on many a weeknight. My Mediterranean Rice Bake is inspired by the flavors of dolmas, grape leaves that are stuffed with rice and seasoned with lemon, dill, and mint. It's refreshing and hearty at the same time, which makes this recipe a great year-round dish.

I'm usually a fan of cooking my own beans, but it's simply easier to use canned chickpeas for this recipe—and that's kind of the point! When looking for canned beans, try to choose ones that are just beans, water, and salt. Some less-expensive brands sneak sulfites and preservatives in there, which are no-nos in my book.

---

2   cups (480 ml) vegetable broth

1   teaspoon onion powder

¼   cup (6 g) fresh dill, chopped

1   tablespoon finely chopped fresh mint

2   (15-ounce/430 g) cans chickpeas, drained and rinsed

1   beefsteak tomato, diced

1   cup (185 g) uncooked brown rice

     Juice of 1 lemon (1 to 2 tablespoons)

1. Preheat the oven to 400°F (205°C) and set a 9 by 13-inch (23 by 33 cm) glass baking dish aside.

2. Put the broth, onion powder, dill, and mint in a medium saucepan. Bring to a boil over high heat.

3. While the liquid is heating, prepare the rest of the casserole: Spread the chickpeas evenly in the base of the baking dish, then top with the tomato and rice.

4. Stir the lemon juice into the broth when it comes to a boil, then pour the liquid over the casserole dish. Use a spatula to evenly distribute the herbs, if any happen to stick in a particular area. Cover the casserole with an oven-safe lid or aluminum foil, then bake on the middle rack of the oven for 60 minutes.

5. Remove from the oven and serve as desired; leftovers will keep in the fridge for up to 5 days.

sweet and smoky chickpea burgers

I've never really been a fan of those meaty imitation burgers . . . probably because I've never had a "real" beef one! Give me a well-seasoned, veggie-filled patty over a soy- or wheat-based one any day and I'm a happy camper.

These chickpea burgers get their deep flavor from roasted red peppers, tomato paste, and plenty of smoked paprika. (If you haven't realized it by now, it's without a doubt my favorite savory spice!) Baking veggie burgers in the oven (versus grilling or pan-frying) is the optimal way to get those crispy burger edges, while still maintaining a soft and chewy burger center. Plus, there's way less hands-on time! This recipe makes six burger patties in total; if you're not cooking for a crowd, freeze a couple to reheat for an easy future lunch or dinner.

FOR THE CHICKPEA BURGERS:

- 2½ cups (420 g) salt-free cooked chickpeas
- ½ cup (95 g) roasted red peppers, drained
- ½ yellow onion, roughly chopped
- Juice of ½ lemon (1 to 3 teaspoons)
- 2 tablespoons tomato paste
- 1 teaspoon smoked paprika
- 1 teaspoon Italian seasoning
- 1 teaspoon pink Himalayan salt
- ½ cup (80 g) brown rice flour
- 1 tablespoon ground flaxseed

FOR SERVING:

- Gluten-free burger buns
- Curly lettuce
- Sliced cucumber
- Everyday Tahini Sauce (page 212)

1. Make the chickpea burgers: Preheat the oven to 400°F (205°C) and line a baking sheet with parchment paper or a silicone mat.

2. Put 1½ cups (255 g) of the chickpeas, the roasted peppers, onion, lemon juice, tomato paste, smoked paprika, Italian seasoning, and salt in a food processor. Process until a thick and relatively smooth paste forms, scraping the sides of the food processor as necessary.

3. Add the brown rice flour and flaxseed to the food processor and pulse to combine. Finally, add the remaining 1 cup (165 g) chickpeas and pulse until they are evenly incorporated into the burger mixture, but still chunky.

4. Slightly wet your hands and divide the dough to form six even burger patties. Round

and flatten each patty with your hands, then place it on the baking sheet. Bake on the middle rack of the oven for 30 minutes, then use a spatula to flip each patty. Return to the top rack of the oven and bake for an additional 10 to 15 minutes, until both sides are golden and crispy.

5. Place each burger on a gluten-free bun and top with lettuce, cucumber, and tahini sauce. Serve warm. Store any leftover patties in the fridge for up to 5 days, or in the freezer for up to 2 months.

crispy veggie flatbreads, two ways

My favorite Three-Ingredient Multipurpose Dough makes yet another tasty appearance . . . this time in the form of a pizza! Well, technically I'm calling them flatbreads because the crust is thinner and crisps up wonderfully in the oven. Technicalities aside, it's still a semi-fluffy circle that you're going to top with sauce and veggies, bake in the oven, and promptly devour.

Speaking of toppings—I've provided two different sauce variations below, but you can really top this dough with whatever you please. Unlike some gluten-free doughs, this one holds up well to heavy decoration, so feel free to really pile it on there and load up the veggies! Make sure you don't forget that sprinkle of nutritional yeast, though—it provides that perfect "cheesy" flavor to these plant-based pizzas.

---

1 batch Three-Ingredient Multipurpose Dough (page 49)

⅛ yellow onion, sliced

3 cremini mushrooms, sliced

2 teaspoons low-sodium tamari

¼ to ½ cup (60 to 120 ml) marinara sauce *or* Kale Pesto (page 219)

¼ cup (50 g) roasted red peppers, sliced

5 Kalamata olives, pitted and cut in half

Nutritional yeast

1. Preheat the oven to 375°F (190°C) and line a baking sheet with parchment paper.

2. Prepare the dough according to the recipe instructions, but roll the dough out to an 9-inch (23 cm) circle instead; it should be about ½ inch (12 mm) thick. Place the dough on the baking sheet, then bake the crust on the middle rack of the oven for 10 minutes.

3. In the meantime, heat a medium-sized sauté pan over medium-high heat, then add the onion, mushrooms, tamari, and 1 tablespoon water; cook until the onions are translucent and the mushrooms shrink, 5 to 7 minutes.

4. Carefully remove the crust from the oven and top with either marinara sauce or pesto. Add the cooked mushrooms and onions, roasted peppers, and olives. Return to the top rack of the oven and bake for 12 to 15 minutes.

5. Remove from the oven, sprinkle with nutritional yeast, then slice, serve, and enjoy.

spaghetti squash lasagna boats

If you haven't noticed by now, I love pasta—there are quite a few recipes for it in this book! However, sometimes it's nice to have a more plant-forward, veggie-heavy dish. That's when spaghetti squash comes in handy. The flesh of this oblong yellow squash magically transforms into spaghetti-like noodles after roasting. They don't have the bounce and chew of a traditional noodle, but they have an incredibly satisfying and almost crunchy texture. Plus they're a great source of fiber, vitamin C, and vitamin B$_6$!

These lasagna boats require more steps and ingredients than other recipes in this book, but I promise they're worth it. First of all, how cute is it to be able to eat your dinner out of a squash? And when it's filled with a creamy spinach and plant-based ricotta filling, then topped with a chunky lentil sauce and drizzle of cashew cream? Now we're talking . . . But enough with the chit-chat, let's get to cooking!

---

2   spaghetti squash

1   cup (240 ml) marinara sauce

1   zucchini, diced

3   cremini mushrooms, finely diced

½   cup (100 g) dried brown lentils

½   teaspoon salt-free Italian seasoning

4   ounces (115 g) baby spinach

1½ cups (235 g) Nut-Free Vegan Ricotta (page 235)

Salt and freshly ground black pepper

½   cup (120 ml) Cashew Cream (page 211; optional)

2   tablespoons finely chopped fresh parsley

Freshly ground black pepper

1. Preheat the oven to 350°F (175°C). Cut the spaghetti squash in half and use a spoon to scoop out the seedy portion in the center. Pour 3 cups (720 ml) water into a large glass baking dish, then arrange the squash cut side up in the dish. Bake for 60 minutes, or until tender.

2. In the meantime, put the marinara sauce, zucchini, mushrooms, lentils, and Italian seasoning in a medium pot with 2 cups (480 ml) water. Bring to a boil over high heat, then reduce the heat to just below medium and simmer, uncovered, for 28 to 30 minutes, until the lentils are tender. Set aside.

3. Carefully remove the cooked squash from the baking dish and increase the oven temperature to 425°F (220°C). Set the water-filled baking dish aside.

4. Put the spinach in a large bowl. Use a fork to scoop the inside of the squash flesh, forming spaghetti-like strands. Be careful to preserve the squash skin itself, as it will be used later as a serving vessel. Add the spaghetti squash strands to the spinach, tossing occasionally with your hands as you scoop. The heat from the squash will wilt the spinach; when it has wilted to about half the size, fold in the ricotta and mix until evenly

incorporated. Season with salt and pepper to taste.

5. Pack each spaghetti squash boat with one-quarter of the spinach and ricotta mixture, then spoon the lentil sauce on top. Drizzle each squash boat with 2 tablespoons cashew cream, then return to the water-filled

baking dish and bake on the top rack of the oven for 10 minutes.

6. Sprinkle each squash boat with chopped parsley and black pepper, then serve warm. Leftovers will keep in the fridge for up to 5 days.

note: If you have leftover Easy Lentil Bolognese (page 144), you can skip the chunky lentil sauce and use that instead!

eat plants, save money

"But I could *never* go vegan, it's way too expensive!" If I had a dollar for every time I heard that, I would be a very rich lady. Unfortunately that's not the way the world works, but fortunately for me, I'm still able to save money . . . by eating a plant-based diet!

Vegan food *can* be expensive—if you're buying tons of mock meats, dairy-free cheeses, energy bars, and processed snacks. Even the trendy, health-centered stuff can add up! But that doesn't have to be the case, especially if you know your way around a kitchen. Here are five easy ways you can eat plants, all while saving your hard-earned coin.

Ditch the labels: Generally speaking, the fewer labels, the better. Whole-plant foods like beans, grains, and seasonal produce will *always* be less expensive than anything that comes in a fancy package. I still buy convenience foods from time to time, but I'd much rather whip up my own easy treats in the kitchen than pay for someone else (or a machine) to do it.

The more the merrier: Buying in bulk has a higher up-front cost, but saves you more in the long run. Don't go buying all of your groceries in large quantities, though— then you'll have food waste, which is a whole separate issue. Think about the nonperishable foods that you go through quickly, and consider buying them in larger quantities from your grocery store or savings club.

Shop seasonally: You'll never find me shelling out for blueberries in January, and for good reason. Not only are they ridiculously expensive, but they also had to travel hundreds of miles to get to my grocery store. Sticking to seasonal produce can save you some major bucks, and it will taste better, too. Enjoy your berries in spring, tomatoes in the summer, and *allll* the squash and potatoes in fall and winter. Not sure what fruits and veggies are in season near you? Visiting your local farmers' market is a great way to find out. A side note: Growing your own herbs can save you a *ton* of money, if you have the time and space.

Don't forget frozen: Did you know that frozen fruits and veggies are preserved at their peak ripeness and can sometimes be *more* nutritious than fresh? Not only that, but they're usually less expensive, and it's easier to find seasonal foods, like berries and corn, year-round. If a fruit or vegetable is being cooked in a recipe, you can almost always substitute it with frozen. It may take a little longer to cook, but only because frozen food tends to release more liquid with heat.

Work with what you've got: There's no need to go out and spend hundreds of bucks at the grocery store if you already have a well-stocked pantry. A recipe calls for maple syrup, but you have agave nectar instead? That'll do. Vegetables are all pretty versatile, too; if it has a similar texture or cooking time, you can usually swap it out for whatever the recipe calls for with no problems.

10 | dessert, please!

I eat dessert every. single. night. The day just doesn't feel complete without a sweet treat at the end of it. Some days it's as simple as dark chocolate and nut butter or a bowl of juicy seasonal fruit, but when I have the time, I like to whip up something special. All of these recipes will satisfy your late-night sweet tooth, but won't leave you with a sugar hangover the next morning.

homemade snickers

lemon bars

I have always loved lemon bars, even as a kid! There's just something about that tangy and sweet combination that hits the dang spot, every time. Traditional lemon bars rely heavily on eggs, white sugar, and butter—but luckily for us, we can achieve a similar consistency (and identical flavor) using arrowroot powder, maple syrup, and soaked cashews!

It's generally acceptable to substitute arrowroot powder for cornstarch or tapioca flour, but it won't work in this recipe. Cornstarch does not thicken well in the oven, and tapioca falls apart with acidic ingredients. Nowadays you can find it in most grocery stores, but it's also easy to purchase online.

FOR THE CRUST:

2   tablespoons ground flaxseed

1   tablespoon grade A maple syrup

1   cup (145 g) raw almonds

1   cup (105 g) rolled oats

½   teaspoon pink Himalayan salt

FOR THE FILLING:

2   cups (290 g) raw cashews, soaked in water for 4–8 hours and drained

½   cup (120 ml) fresh lemon juice (from about 3 lemons)

    Grated zest of 1 lemon

¼   cup plus 3 tablespoons (105 ml) grade A maple syrup

1   teaspoon vanilla extract

2   tablespoons arrowroot powder

⅛   teaspoon ground turmeric (optional, for color)

¼   teaspoon pink Himalayan salt

1. Preheat the oven to 350°F (175°C) and line a 9-inch (23 cm) square baking pan with parchment paper so that there is 1 to 2 inches extra to grab on two sides.

2. Make the crust: Combine the flaxseed, maple syrup, and 5 tablespoons (75 ml) water in a small bowl; whisk well, then set aside for 5 minutes to thicken to an egg-like consistency.

3. Put the almonds, oats, and salt in a high-speed blender or food processor and process at low speed until finely ground. Add the thickened flaxseed mixture, then pulse until a thick dough forms. Use your fingers to firmly and evenly press the crust into the base of the pan. Bake on the middle rack of the oven for 10 minutes.

4. Meanwhile, make the filling: Quickly rinse the blender, then put the cashews, lemon juice, lemon zest, maple syrup, vanilla, arrowroot powder, turmeric (if using), and salt in the container. Blend on high speed until smooth and creamy, 45 to 60 seconds. Pour the lemon filling over the baked crust and use a spatula to even out the top. Return to the oven and bake for 18 to 20 minutes, until the edges of the bar are firm and pull away from the pan. The bars may look slightly runny in the center, but the filling will thicken as it cools.

5. Let the bars cool completely in the pan, then use the parchment paper to cleanly remove them and transfer to a flat surface. Cut into nine squares, then serve as desired. Leftovers will keep at room temperature for up to 3 days, or in the fridge for up to 1 week.

strawberry rhubarb crumble bars

These bars = the perfect spring dessert. Sweet strawberries meld with tart rhubarb for a juicy and refreshing filling while oats, almond flour, and maple syrup combine to make an irresistibly crunchy crumble top.

It's best to use fresh strawberries for this recipe as they are generally sweeter, but frozen will work in a pinch. If you do go frozen, you'll have to simmer the filling for a few minutes longer to get rid of the extra water. These crumble bars are best served while still warm—topping them with a scoop of dairy-free vanilla ice cream is an absolute dream. The bars will soften over time as they sit on your countertop, but I still enjoy them this way as well.

FOR THE STRAWBERRY RHUBARB FILLING:

- 1½ cups (225 g) sliced fresh strawberries
- 1½ cups (195 g) thinly sliced fresh rhubarb
- ⅓ cup (75 ml) grade A maple syrup
- 1 teaspoon vanilla extract
- Pinch of pink Himalayan salt

FOR THE DOUGH AND CRUMBLE TOPPING:

- 1 cup (100 g) blanched almond flour
- ½ cup (55 g) tapioca flour
- 1½ cups (160 g) quick-cooking oats
- ½ teaspoon baking powder
- ½ teaspoon pink Himalayan salt
- ¾ cup (200 g) unsalted almond butter
- ⅔ cup (165 ml) grade A maple syrup

1. Preheat the oven to 350°F (175°C) and line an 8-inch (20 cm) square baking pan with parchment paper.

2. Make the strawberry rhubarb filling: Put the strawberries, rhubarb, maple syrup, vanilla, and salt in a medium pot over high heat. When the mixture starts to bubble, reduce the heat to medium and simmer for 8 to 12 minutes, stirring the mixture frequently to ensure nothing burns or sticks to the pan. Set aside to cool slightly.

3. Make the dough and crumble topping: Put the almond flour, tapioca flour, oats, baking powder, and salt in a large bowl and mix until evenly incorporated. Stir the almond butter and maple syrup together in small bowl, then add this mixture to the dry ingredients. Stir well until no dry lumps are left—the mixture should be pretty thick!

4. Press half of the "dough" into the bottom of the baking tin, then pour the berry filling on top. Use your hands to evenly crumble the remaining dough over the top of the fruit.

5. Bake on the middle rack of the oven until the crumb topping is crisp and slightly browned, 27 to 30 minutes. Transfer the pan to a wire rack and let cool completely before slicing in the pan. Serve as desired; leftovers will keep at room temperature for up to 3 days.

fudgy tahini raspberry brownies

If you like your brownies fudgy and decadent, this is the recipe for you! Tahini adds a complex nutty element (plus a good source of calcium), while tart raspberries serve as a nice counterbalance to the rich chocolate flavor. As in my No-Bake Cosmic Brownies (page 114), I use cacao powder—you can substitute regular cocoa powder, but it will be a little more bitter. These brownies are made from wholesome ingredients, but are definitely on the indulgent side. That's one of the many reasons why I love them— you only need one to feel full and satisfied, and it won't leave you with a sugar hangover later.

These brownies, like most, are best devoured straight out of the oven. However, they'll keep for up to 5 days on your counter. For ultimate enjoyment, I suggest reheating them in a toaster oven or air-fryer for a few minutes—then serve with a nice, tall glass of cold almond milk.

2	tablespoons ground flaxseed
1	cup (105 g) quick-cooking oats, blended to make oat flour
¼	cup (26 g) cacao powder
½	teaspoon baking powder
½	teaspoon pink Himalayan salt
¾	cup (180 ml) unsweetened nondairy milk
1	cup (250 g) tahini
¾	cup (120 g) coconut sugar
1	teaspoon vanilla extract
½	cup (110 g) dairy-free chocolate chips
3	ounces fresh raspberries

1. Preheat the oven to 350°F (175°C) and line a 9-inch (23 cm) square baking pan with parchment paper. Combine the flaxseed with 5 tablespoons (75 ml) water in a small bowl, then set aside for 5 minutes to thicken to an egg-like consistency.

2. Put the oat flour, cacao powder, baking powder, and salt in a large bowl and whisk until well combined. Form a well in the center of the mixture, then add the milk, ¾ cup (190 g) of the tahini, the coconut sugar, vanilla, and thickened flax mixture. Mix until a thick batter forms, then fold in half of the chocolate chips and half of the raspberries.

3. Pour the batter into the baking tin and spread it around evenly with a spatula. Drizzle the remaining tahini over the top of the batter, then use a butter knife to swirl everything around. Sprinkle the reserved chocolate chips on top, then gently press the remaining raspberries into the batter.

4. Bake for 28 to 30 minutes, then let cool in the pan for 10 to 15 minutes before removing. Transfer the pan to a wire rack and let cool completely before slicing in the pan. Store any leftovers in a container with a loose-fitting lid at room temperature for up to 5 days.

note: Tahini can have a strong taste—I personally love it, but if you'd like things on the milder side, swap ¼ cup (65 g) of it with another nut or seed butter instead.

cinnamon-sugar donuts

You know what they say . . . eat more (w)hole foods for optimal health. And who doesn't love a good ol' donut?! These baked cinnamon-sugar donuts are a lighter take on the classic, plus they use coconut sugar instead of refined table sugar; it has higher levels of iron, zinc, and calcium. I know some people don't consider baked donuts to be real donuts, but I've always preferred them over the fried, yeasty varieties. Give me a moist and fluffy cake donut over that icky pink-frosted, sprinkled stuff any day!

I use silicone donut molds to make this recipe so I don't have to grease the pan—you can buy them online, or bake these into muffins instead. Note that silicone molds can be a little flimsy, especially after you fill them. I like to place mine on a baking sheet to make them easier to put in and take out of the oven.

FOR THE DONUTS:

- 2 tablespoons ground flaxseed
- 1½ cups (155 g) quick-cooking oats, blended to make oat flour
- ½ teaspoon baking powder
- ½ teaspoon baking soda
- 1½ teaspoons ground cinnamon
- ½ teaspoon pink Himalayan salt
- 1 cup (240 ml) nondairy milk
- ½ cup (130 g) unsalted almond butter
- ½ cup (75 g) coconut sugar
- 1 tablespoon apple cider vinegar
- ½ teaspoon vanilla extract

FOR THE CINNAMON-SUGAR TOPPING:

- ⅓ cup (55 g) coconut sugar
- ½ teaspoon ground cinnamon
- 2 tablespoons nondairy milk (for brushing)

1. Make the donuts: Preheat the oven to 350°F (175°C). Combine the flaxseed with 5 tablespoons (75 ml) water in a medium bowl, then set aside for 5 minutes to thicken to an egg-like consistency. In a separate, larger bowl, combine the oat flour, baking powder, baking soda, cinnamon, and salt and mix well.

2. Add the milk, almond butter, coconut sugar, vinegar, and vanilla to the bowl with the thickened flax mixture. Mix well, then add the wet ingredients to the bowl of dry ingredients. Stir until no lumps remain.

3. Evenly divide the batter among twelve donut molds, then smooth out the tops using a small spatula. Bake for 25 minutes, then let stand in the pan for 3 minutes. Carefully pull the edges of the silicone molds to loosen the donuts, then remove them and transfer to a wire rack to let cool completely.

4. Make the cinnamon-sugar topping: Mix the coconut sugar and cinnamon together in a small bowl with a wide base. When the donuts are cool, lightly brush each side with milk, then dip into the cinnamon-sugar mixture. Store any leftovers in a container with a loose-fitting lid at room temperature for up to 5 days.

note: Make this recipe nut-free by using tahini or sunflower butter in place of almond butter.

salted caramel chocolate chip cookies

I always like to keep a jar of Salted Caramel Sauce on hand, and one day I had the brilliant idea of using it as the liquid in cookies. Here it acts as a three-for-one, adding natural sweetness, creaminess, and a subtle saltiness that, in my opinion, should be required in all baked goods. Seriously, people! Adding salt to your baked goods won't make them salty—in fact, it actually rounds out the flavor and allows you to experience the sweet flavors more fully. If a dessert recipe doesn't call for a touch of salt, I simply don't trust it.

Some people may be more inclined to call these cookies soft shortbreads; they aren't overly sweet, and the oat flour creates a hearty, almost creamy bite. Using a dairy-free chocolate in the 65% cacao range will help to make them sweeter, if you prefer. Whatever you do, use a chocolate bar, not chips! Most chocolate chips are blended with wax, which prevents them from melting and getting all ooey gooey. I also think the itty-bitty flecks of chopped chocolate spread throughout the cookies makes them look that much better. The tahini in this recipe provides an additional layer of nuttiness and a unique caramel-esque flavor. I wouldn't skip it, but you can replace it with cashew butter if you must.

¾ cup (180 ml) Salted Caramel Sauce (page 215)

½ cup (120 g) tahini

2 tablespoons coconut sugar

1 teaspoon vanilla extract

1 teaspoon baking powder

1½ cups (155 g) quick-cooking oats, blended to make oat flour

1.76 ounces (50 g) dairy-free chocolate, chopped

Maldon or flaky sea salt

1. Preheat the oven to 350°F (175°C) and line a baking sheet with parchment paper or a silicone mat.

2. Combine the caramel sauce, tahini, coconut sugar, vanilla, and baking powder in a large bowl. Add the oat flour and mix until no lumps remain. Fold in the chocolate until evenly combined.

3. Scoop 3-tablespoon-sized balls of dough into your hands and gently press them into round cookie shapes; they will not spread much with baking. Place the cookies on the baking sheet, then bake on the middle rack of the oven for 12 minutes. Remove from the oven, sprinkle with salt, then let sit for 3 minutes before using a spatula to transfer to a wire rack to cool completely.

4. Serve as desired; leftovers will keep at room temperature for up to 3 days.

note: If you find that the batter starts to stick to your hands, rinse them off and pat them almost dry, but keep them slightly damp—this prevents the stickies, and also makes the dough much easier to shape.

homemade snickers

Snickers were my all-time favorite candy bars as a kid—I would literally trade all of my Halloween candy stash with my brothers just to have more of that chewy, crunchy, nougat-y goodness. These homemade candy bars taste so realistic that people sometimes don't believe me when I tell them that they're gluten-free, refined sugar–free, and made with only six plant-based ingredients. If it weren't for the recipe I'm giving you now, you probably wouldn't believe me either.

One (optional) ingredient that I want to call out is the maca powder. This Peruvian root is one of the more popular superfoods that's popped up lately, and for good reason. It can help your body cope with stress while also giving you a natural boost of energy, plus it has a sweet, malty flavor reminiscent of caramel. Because it's becoming more commonly used, you can find well-priced options at some grocery stores—but if you can't find it, don't sweat it. These bars are perfectly delicious without it.

1   packed cup (265 g) Medjool dates, pitted

2   tablespoons natural peanut butter

1   teaspoon vanilla extract

1   teaspoon maca powder (optional)

¼   teaspoon pink Himalayan salt

⅔   cup (35 g) quick-cooking or rolled oats, blended to make oat flour

⅓   cup (50 g) dry-roasted salted peanuts

4   ounces (115 g) dairy-free chocolate, chopped

note: If you don't have mini loaf pans, don't worry! Another small bread loaf pan (or small glass storage container) will work just fine.

1. Line a four-cavity 5¾ by 3-inch (14.5 by 7.5 cm) loaf pan with parchment paper and set aside.

2. Put the dates in a medium bowl and cover with hot water; let soak for 10 minutes, then drain. Discard the water, or save it for smoothies and tea!

3. Put the dates, peanut butter, vanilla, maca powder (if using), and salt in a food processor. Process until the mixture is thick and smooth, stopping to scrape down the sides of the bowl, if necessary. Set this "caramel" aside.

4. Without wiping out the bowl of the food processor, add the oat flour and ¼ cup (60 ml) of the caramel. Process for 1 minute, or until a slightly sticky "nougat" forms that will hold together when pinched. Firmly press the nougat into the mini loaf pan, then use a spatula to spread the remaining caramel evenly over the top. Sprinkle the "loaves" with peanuts, then use your fingers to gently press them into the caramel so they stick.

5. Freeze the pan for 60 to 90 minutes, until the bars are nice and firm. Remove the bars from the pan and use a sharp knife to slice into rectangles 1½ inches (4 cm) wide. Line a baking pan or large plate with parchment paper, and return the bars to the freezer while you melt the chocolate.

6. Put the chocolate in a wide microwave-safe bowl and microwave at 30-second intervals, stirring in between. When the chocolate is about 75 percent melted, stir with a spatula until completely melted. Moving quickly, place one candy bar in the bowl of chocolate and use two forks to flip the bar until it is coated in chocolate on all sides. Allow any excess chocolate to drip off before transferring it to parchment paper; repeat with the remaining bars.

7. Place the bars in the fridge for 5 to 10 minutes, until set.

Serve as desired; leftovers will keep in the fridge for up to 10 days, or can be frozen for up to 2 months. If storing in the freezer, allow the bars to sit on the counter for 5 to 7 minutes before enjoying.

golden milk mango popsicles

I feel like many of us group popsicles into the "kid-only" dessert category. Those sugar-filled, artificially dyed, plastic-wrapped icicles? Yeah, I'm ready to leave those behind. But a creamy, dreamy popsicle made of fresh fruit, coconut milk, and warming spices? I'm *totally* ready to get down with that. These mango popsicles are a refreshing year-round treat, especially after a warm bowl of Curried Carrot Soup (page 67) or Chickpea Tikka Masala (page 143)

You will need a popsicle mold in order to make this recipe; I have tried my fair share, and find that silicone-based molds work better than the hard plastic ones. The stretchy nature of the rubber makes it easier to loosen the popsicles before removing them from the mold. Be sure to carefully run room-temperature water around the outside of the mold, too, or you'll be in for a fantastic pre-dessert arm workout.

1½ cups (215 g) frozen chopped mango

1 (13½-ounce/400 ml) can full-fat coconut milk

⅓ cup (80 ml) grade A maple syrup

1-inch (2.5 cm) knob of fresh ginger, peeled

Juice of ½ small lemon (about 2 teaspoons)

1½ teaspoons ground turmeric

1 teaspoon ground cinnamon

¼ teaspoon ground cardamom

Pinch of pink Himalayan salt

1. Put the mango, coconut milk, maple syrup, ginger, lemon juice, turmeric, cinnamon, cardamom, and salt in a high-speed blender and process until smooth and creamy, 45 to 60 seconds.

2. Use a funnel to pour the mixture into your popsicle molds, leaving a little room at the top to allow the mixture to expand as it freezes. Place a popsicle stick in the center of each mold and seal the mold as necessary. Place the popsicles on a level surface in the freezer and freeze for at least 4 hours, preferably overnight.

3. Carefully run room-temperature water over the outside of the mold to loosen the popsicles, then remove each popsicle from the mold. Serve; store any leftovers in a sealed container in the freezer for up to 2 months.

blueberry cardamom cheesecake

My favorite spice and fruit combination strikes again, this time in the form of a plant-based cheesecake! The no-bake, dairy-free filling is made from a combination of soaked cashews, coconut milk, and Medjool dates for a thick, creamy, and indulgent bite. The crust contains raw almonds, but if you have a nut allergy you can replace them with unsweetened shredded coconut.

A few notes on equipment: You will need both a high-speed blender with a tamper and a springform pan for this recipe. If you don't have a high-end blender, make the cheesecake crust in a food processor. However, you will need to make the filling in a blender; the cashews will not blend properly in a food processor, and you will be left with a chunky (albeit delicious) cake. The springform pan is optional, but highly recommended. If you don't have one you can attempt to line a cake pan or glass dish with parchment paper, but this usually proves tricky and makes the sides of the cake lumpy. If you're having trouble removing the cheesecake from the base of your springform pan, carefully slide a wide knife under the crust to easily separate it from the bottom.

FOR THE CRUST:

- 1 cup (105 g) quick-cooking oats
- ½ cup (75 g) raw almonds
- Pinch of pink Himalayan salt
- ⅓ packed cup (90 g) Medjool dates, pitted

note: If you forget to soak your cashews, cover them in boiling water and let sit for 10 minutes, then drain and use.

FOR THE BLUEBERRY CARDAMOM FILLING:

- 1 cup (140 g) raw cashews, soaked in water for at least 4 hours and drained
- 1 (13½-ounce/400 ml) can full-fat coconut milk
- 1 cup (135 g) frozen blueberries
- ⅓ packed cup (90 g) Medjool dates, pitted
- Grated zest and juice of 1 small lemon (1 to 2 tablespoons)
- 2 teaspoons vanilla extract
- 1½ teaspoons ground cardamom
- ¾ teaspoon pink Himalayan salt

1. Make the crust: Put the oats, almonds, and salt in a high-speed blender and pulse until a fine flour forms. Use your hands to break up the dates into small pieces, then add them to the blender, along with 2 tablespoons water. Blend at medium-low speed, using a tamper to "mix" the dough while it blends. When the dough forms a thick, sticky paste, use a spatula to remove it from the blender and firmly press it into the base of a 9-inch (23 cm) springform pan. Place the crust in

the freezer while you prepare the filling.

2. Make the blueberry cardamom filling: Quickly rinse out the blender, then add the cashews, coconut milk, blueberries, dates, lemon zest, lemon juice, vanilla, cardamom, and salt. Blend at high speed

until a thick and even batter forms, 60 to 90 seconds. Pour the filling into the springform pan and use a spatula to smooth out the top. Lift the springform pan a few centimeters off of the countertop, then gently "drop" it several times, to remove any air bubbles.

3. Place the cheesecake in the freezer until firm, at least 4 hours. When firm, remove from the freezer and let sit for 10 minutes before slicing and serving. Store leftovers in an airtight container in the freezer, where they will last for up to 2 months.

coco-mint chip shake

Mint and chocolate—it's either a love it or hate it kind of thing. I, for one, am a pretty big fan. Not only do I love the taste, but it's also kind of nostalgic for me. My dad used to eat a giant bowl of mint chocolate chip ice cream for dessert every night, without fail. He doesn't do it anymore (since going vegan), but hey, Dad—maybe you can give this a try?

The zucchini in this recipe isn't really for health purposes, but I guess that's just an added bonus. It's mostly in the shake mix to add color and volume, without the need for artificial dyes or thickeners. Don't let this sneaky squash fool you, though—this shake is rich, indulgent, and definitely qualifies as dessert, not a breakfast smoothie. The peppermint extract helps to balance out the cool and creamy coconut for an all-around refreshing and mouthwatering treat. You can use either cacao nibs or chocolate chips in this recipe; the former is crunchy and dark, while the latter is softer and sweet.

¾ cup (180 ml) coconut cream

½ cup (60 ml) maple syrup

1 small zucchini

½ teaspoon vanilla extract

1 teaspoon peppermint extract

1 cup (240 ml) nondairy milk, plus more as desired

3 tablespoons cacao nibs or mini dairy-free chocolate chips

note: Some grocery stores sell cans of coconut cream, while others only sell regular coconut milk. Regardless, it always helps to refrigerate your cans of cream/milk before scooping out the cream. Unfortunately, each brand also contains different amounts of cream and liquid—you may be okay with just one can, but I'd recommend chilling two just in case.

1. Open the can(s) of coconut cream and scoop out the firm, white portion. Discard the clear liquid (or save it for smoothies!). Put ¼ cup (60 ml) of the coconut cream, the maple syrup, zucchini, vanilla, and peppermint extract in a blender. Blend on high speed until smooth and creamy, 45 to 50 seconds. Use a spatula to transfer the mixture into ice cube molds, then place in the freezer for at least 6 hours, preferably overnight. Place the rest of the coconut cream in the fridge—you'll use it later.

2. The next day, put the frozen ice cubes in a blender, along with the remaining coconut cream and the milk. Blend for 30 seconds on low speed to help break up the ice, then process on the highest speed until smooth and creamy. If you'd like to loosen the shake, add more milk as desired. Add the cacao nibs or chocolate chips to the blender and pulse to combine. Pour into serving glasses and serve immediately.

11 | let's get saucy

This chapter contains all of the
sauces, dressings, and various
other condiments that you've
seen throughout the book. Why are
they in a separate chapter, you ask? Because I
don't want you to limit yourself! Sure, they go well with
one or two of the recipes in this book, but they're just
as great on top of your favorite salad, spread on toast, or
drizzled over a weeknight veggie bowl. So go get saucy,
my friend!

miso tahini gravy

cashews, two ways

Cashews are pretty much a vegan staple. The creamy, neutral-flavored nuts soften after soaking in water for only a few hours, making them the perfect base for a plant-based twist on practically any food that's traditionally made with dairy. Because they're so versatile, I almost always have either a Mason jar of soaked cashews or a bottle of cashew cream tucked away in my fridge.

The cashew cream is a great substitute for heavy cream and sour cream. You'll find it in Herby Tofu Scramble (page 42), Creamy Corn Chowder (page 75), and Dill-icious Mashed Potatoes (page 148), among other recipes. The cashew mayo is a great soy-free and egg-free alternative to mayonnaise. I use it in Rosemary Potato Salad (page 96), but you can use this creamy, slightly tangy spread anywhere and everywhere you'd normally use mayo.

Hands-on time:
5 MINUTES

Makes about 1½ cups (360 ml)

cashew cream

1 cup (145 g) raw cashews, soaked in water for at least 4 hours and drained

¼ teaspoon pink Himalayan salt

½ teaspoon nutritional yeast (optional)

1. Put the cashews, salt, and nutritional yeast (if using) in a high-speed blender with ¾ cup 180 ml) water. Process until smooth and creamy, 45 to 60 seconds. Store in an airtight container in the fridge for up to 2 weeks.

note: This cashew cream has a thick, drizzle-able consistency straight out of the blender, but will thicken to more of a spread in the fridge. If you are planning to use it at a later date, blend the cashews with 1 cup (240 ml) water instead.

Hands-on time:
5 MINUTES

Makes about 1¼ cups (300 ml)

cashew mayo

1 cup (145 g) raw cashews, soaked in water overnight and drained

1 teaspoon fresh lemon juice

1 teaspoon distilled white vinegar

½ teaspoon nutritional yeast

¼ teaspoon Dijon mustard

¾ teaspoon pink Himalayn salt

1. Put the cashews, lemon juice, vinegar, nutritional yeast, mustard, and salt in a high-speed blender with 6 tablespoons (90 ml) water. Blend until smooth and creamy, 45 to 60 seconds, scraping the sides of the blender with a spatula if necessary. Store in an airtight container in the fridge for up to 2 weeks.

note: You will need either a high-speed blender with a tamper or a bullet blender for this recipe. If everything does not come together smoothly, add water in 1-tablespoon increments until your desired texture is reached.

tahini sauce, three ways

There's a reason I decided to (partially) dedicate this book to tahini—it's *so* underrated! This complex, nutty, and slightly earthy sesame spread is a great source of calcium, plant protein, and dietary fiber. It's classically used in hummus (page 106), but I like to break the rules often and use it in both savory and sweet foods, without restraint.

The following tahini sauces are pantry staples for me; I gravitate toward a giant, veggie-packed salad at the end of the day, and I love how I can whip up one of these creamy, flavor-filled dressings in no time flat. While some tahini can have a bitter taste, the best varieties are silky, smooth, and only slightly nutty. Look for unhulled, organic tahini—Soom Foods is a women-owned, US-based company that makes a great tahini; otherwise, the less English on the bottle, the better.

FOR ROSEMARY TAHINI SAUCE:

- ½ cup (115 g) tahini
- 1 tablespoon finely chopped fresh rosemary
- 1 large clove garlic, finely minced
- ¼ cup (60 ml) fresh lemon juice (from about 2 lemons)
- ½ teaspoon freshly ground black pepper
- ½ teaspoon pink Himalayan salt

FOR EVERYDAY TAHINI SAUCE:

- ½ cup (115 g) tahini
- ¼ cup (60 ml) fresh lemon juice (from about 2 lemons)
- ¼ teaspoon smoked paprika
- ½ teaspoon ground cumin
- ½ teaspoon garlic powder
- ½ teaspoon pink Himalayan salt

FOR TAHINI DIJON SAUCE:

- ½ cup (115 g) tahini
- 2 tablespoons Dijon mustard
- 1 tablespoon grade A maple syrup
- ¼ teaspoon pink Himalayan salt

1. Put all the ingredients in a medium bowl and whisk together to form a thick paste.

2. Pour ¼ cup (60 ml) water into the bowl as you whisk it into the mixture. Slowly add an additional ¼ to ½ cup (60 to 120 ml) water while you mix the dressing vigorously, until it reaches your desired consistency.

3. Serve as desired. Leftovers will keep in the fridge for up to 2 weeks and will thicken over time.

salted caramel sauce

This simple sauce might only be made with three ingredients, but it could easily go up against anything store-bought or restaurant-made—including versions using refined sugars and butter. The secret ingredient? Miso paste! This funky ferment is actually really mild in flavor, so all you taste is a subtle saltiness that perfectly complements the sweetness of the coconut sugar. You can use it in place of caramel sauce in practically any recipe—you'll use it in Salted Caramel French Toast Casserole (page 53) and Salted Caramel Chocolate Chip Cookies (page 198), but it's just as delicious over ice cream, brownies, or pancakes. Heck, you can even use it as a fruit dip! The sauce itself will keep in the fridge for up to two weeks—I always have some on hand.

1   cup (155 g) coconut sugar

1   cup (145 g) raw cashews, soaked in water for at least 4 hours and drained

2   tablespoons yellow miso paste

1. Blend the coconut sugar, cashews, miso paste, and 1 cup (240 ml) water together in a high-speed blender for 45 seconds, until smooth and creamy. Pour the sauce into a nonstick saucepan over medium-high heat. Simmer the sauce until it has thickened and coats the back of a spoon, 5 to 7 minutes—keep in mind that it will also thicken as it cools. Whisk frequently to ensure that nothing sticks to the bottom of the pan.

2. Transfer the sauce to a sealable jar or container and let it cool completely before storing it in the fridge for up to 2 weeks. You may need to loosen the cooled caramel slightly before using; simply microwave it for about 10 seconds or heat it over low heat in a pot.

notes: Yellow miso adds a wonderful deep, complex flavor to this sauce. You can use chickpea miso if you'd prefer, but don't skip it! It should be available in the refrigerated section of most grocery stores near the tofu.

If you have a tree nut allergy (or don't have a powerful blender), you can replace the cashews with 1¼ cups (300 ml) full-fat coconut milk and simmer the mixture for 10 to 12 minutes.

miso tahini gravy

This gravy is bursting with umami flavor and has a unique nuttiness to it, thanks to the simple combination of miso paste, tahini, and toasted nutritional yeast. It's not like those traditional stock-based or mushroom-based versions, but I love it just the same. Whether you serve it alongside a Sweet Potato and Kale Skillet (page 46), drizzle it over some Dill-icious Mashed Potatoes (page 148), or use it as the unifying sauce at your next fall holiday meal, this liquid gold is sure to have you coming back for more.

Miso paste adds some much-needed saltiness and flavor complexity here, but it can be finicky to work with as it separates easily with heat—just make sure to remove the pot from the heat before you whisk in the miso. I prefer to use a mild yellow miso here, but chickpea miso will also work if you have a soy allergy.

½ cup (40 g) nutritional yeast

1 tablespoon brown rice flour or other gluten-free flour

1 cup (240 ml) vegetable broth

⅓ cup (90 g) tahini

½ teaspoon freshly ground black pepper

3 tablespoons yellow miso paste

Pink Himalayan salt

1. Heat a medium pot over medium heat, then add the nutritional yeast and brown rice flour. Toast for 3 to 5 minutes, stirring frequently. The nutritional yeast will darken in color and release a fragrant "smoke" when toasted.

2. Add the broth, tahini, pepper, and ½ cup (120 ml) water, whisking rapidly to combine. Raise the heat to medium-high until the mixture begins to bubble, then reduce the heat to low and simmer for 1 to 2 minutes, stirring frequently. Remove from the heat, then rapidly stir in the miso paste; taste the mixture and season with additional pepper and salt, if necessary.

3. Serve immediately; store any leftovers in the fridge for up to 7 days. This gravy will thicken and separate as it cools, so I suggest reheating with extra vegetable broth and whisking everything together until it smooths out again.

kale pesto

While dairy- and oil-free pesto may seem like an impossibility to many, I promise that this delivers on taste, texture, and creaminess. The secret? Toasting both the nuts and the nutritional yeast for extra depth of flavor. I like to use a combination of pine nuts and macadamias for that rich, buttery taste you'd normally get with olive oil and Parmesan. Replacing both with pumpkin seeds will also work just fine, if you happen to have a nut allergy.

Adding a few leaves of kale with the basil gives this pesto an extra boost of color, fiber, and antioxidants, without any noticeable taste. It's a perfect way to sneak some greens into a picky person's diet! This pesto is more of a thick spread than runny sauce, which only adds to its versatility. You can toss it with your favorite pasta (page 157), but it also works well on avocado toast (page 23), as a pizza sauce (page 183), or as a dip for crudités and crackers.

⅓ cup (45 g) pine nuts

½ cup (65 g) macadamia nuts, cut in half

⅓ cup (25 g) nutritional yeast

Juice of 1 large lemon (2-3 tablespoons)

½ teaspoon lemon zest

4 large leaves kale, stems and tough center ribs removed

2 packed cups (70 g) fresh basil

2 to 3 cloves garlic

¼ teaspoon red pepper flakes, plus more to taste

½ teaspoon pink Himalayan salt

1. Put the pine nuts and macadamia nuts in a nonstick pan over medium heat. Toast the nuts for 3½ minutes, stirring frequently with a spatula to ensure all sides cook evenly. Transfer to a high-speed blender or food processor, then return the pan to the heat.

2. Toast the nutritional yeast in the pan for 45 to 50 seconds using the same process. When it turns a darker golden color and starts to smoke, remove it from the heat and add it to the blender as well.

3. Add the lemon juice, lemon zest, kale, basil, garlic, red pepper flakes, salt, and ½ cup (120 ml) water to the blender, then process on high speed until smooth and creamy. For thinner pesto, add additional water to the blender or food processor in 1-tablespoon increments, until the sauce reaches your desired level of thickness.

4. Serve as desired; store leftovers in a sealed container in the fridge for up to 5 days, or the freezer for up to 2 months.

creamy avocado dressing

This salad dressing is creamy without the need for any oil, all thanks to avocado! I love the smooth texture and mouthfeel avocado brings to dressings and dips. This recipe in particular is subtly spiced, which makes it a great dressing for almost any combination of leafy greens and crunchy things. You can also use it as a dip for veggies, crackers, or chips.

If you'd like your dressing to be on the thicker side, use only ⅓ cup (80 ml) water; this is the perfect consistency for dipping or massaging into heartier leafy greens, like kale. If you'd like your dressing to be a bit runnier, simply double the water to thin it out.

1 large Hass avocado, pitted

Juice of 1 small lemon
(1 to 2 tablespoons)

¼ teaspoon ground cumin

⅛ teaspoon ground cayenne

¼ teaspoon pink Himalayan salt, plus more to taste

Scoop the flesh of the avocado into a bullet or high-speed blender, then add the lemon juice, cumin, cayenne, salt, and ⅓ cup (80 ml) water. Process until smooth and creamy, 15 to 30 seconds. If you would like your dressing to be more pourable, add an additional ⅓ cup (80 ml) water to the blender and process again. Serve as desired; leftovers can be refrigerated in an airtight container for up to 3 days, but will darken over time as the avocado oxidizes.

roasted cherry balsamic vinaigrette

This vinaigrette is the perfect balance of sweet and tangy. Cherries contribute a wonderful tart flavor to the dressing—and you can use either fresh or frozen for this recipe. I actually prefer to use frozen, because they are already pitted, pretty widely available, and usually more affordable than fresh. The addition of a Medjool dates helps to balance everything out with a subtle sweetness, while still keeping everything refined sugar-free. If your date is on the harder side, soak it in hot water for five minutes to soften it up, then drain and use as directed.

This dressing is used in the cherry and arugula salad (page 87), but can be used in place of balsamic vinaigrette in practically any recipe. It also makes a fun marinade for roasted tempeh or portobello mushroom steaks!

---

1   cup (130 g) fresh or frozen cherries, pitted

¼   cup (60 ml) balsamic vinegar

1   small clove garlic, peeled

½   cup (120 ml) nondairy milk

1   large Medjool date, pitted

½   teaspoon pink Himalayan salt
    Freshly cracked black pepper

1. Preheat the oven to 425°F (220°C) and line a baking sheet with a silicone mat or parchment paper.

2. Spread the cherries evenly across the baking sheet, then bake on the middle rack of the oven for 10 to 15 minutes.

3. Transfer the cherries to a blender, along with the vinegar, garlic, milk, date, salt, and pepper to taste. Blend on high speed for 45 to 60 seconds, until a smooth dressing forms and no date chunks remain.

4. Serve as desired; leftovers will keep in the fridge for up to 5 days.

note: If you are using frozen cherries, roast them straight from the freezer—no need to thaw first!

chimichurri dressing

Chimichurri is an Argentinian sauce usually made from fresh herbs, olive oil, and garlic. It's often used as a marinade for protein sources, or as a condiment for fresh bread or roasted vegetables. It's not spicy in terms of heat, but it does have a strong, intense, and fresh flavor thanks to heaps of parsley and oregano.

This oil-free version of chimichurri relies on many of the same ingredients, but I use olive brine (the salty liquid from a jar of olives) in place of olive oil to provide a similar flavor. Castelvetrano olives have the best brine for this recipe—they have a rich, buttery flavor that most olives lack. You can use the sauce and the actual olives in the Chimichurri Quinoa Salad (page 91), so I'd recommend stocking up on a jar or two. If you can't find them at your grocery store, another variety of green olive will work as well.

1	bunch fresh flat-leaf parsley, roughly chopped (about 1½ cups/30 g)
¼	cup (12 g) loosely packed fresh oregano leaves
4	cloves garlic, peeled
¼	cup (60 ml) red wine vinegar
¼	cup (60 ml) olive brine
¼	teaspoon red chile flakes (optional, for added spice)
¼	teaspoon pink Himalayan salt

1. Put the parsley, oregano, garlic, vinegar, olive brine, chile flakes, and salt in a food processor. Process for 45 to 60 seconds, or until the herbs are finely chopped, scraping the sides of the device with a spatula if necessary.

2. Use as desired. This dressing is best enjoyed fresh, but can be stored in the fridge for up to 5 days.

healthy orange sauce

While not a traditional Asian sauce, I think most of us can admit that we quite enjoy that sweet, sticky orange sauce that coats many a Chinese takeout dish. This one tastes just as yummy as the classic, but is made without any refined sugars or questionable preservatives! It technically won't keep as long in your fridge as the bottled stuff, but I think you'll find that you use it up way before its expiration date anyway.

I strongly recommend using fresh-squeezed orange juice in this recipe; you can make it yourself, or buy the fresh-pressed variety from your local grocery store. Most store-bought orange juice is flash pasteurized, meaning it's rapidly heated and cooled before being packaged to give it a longer shelf life. This, while great for long-term storage, drastically affects the flavor of orange juice—the final product is much less floral, less sweet, and more bitter. I've made this sauce with both forms of OJ, and definitely notice a difference when I use fresh.

---

1   cup (240 ml) fresh orange juice, with pulp (from about 2 large navel oranges)

1   teaspoon grated orange zest

½   cup (120 ml) maple syrup

¼   cup (60 ml) plus 1 tablespoon reduced-sodium tamari

¼   cup (60 ml) rice vinegar

3   cloves garlic, peeled

¾   yellow onion

1-inch (2.5 cm) knob of fresh ginger, peeled

Pinch of red chile flakes (optional)

1   tablespoon arrowroot powder

1. Put the orange juice, orange zest, maple syrup, tamari, vinegar, garlic, onion, ginger, red chile flakes, and arrowroot powder in a high-speed blender. Blend on high speed for 30 seconds, until a uniform sauce forms.

2. Pour the sauce into a small pot and bring to a boil over high heat, whisking occasionally. When it's bubbling, reduce the heat to medium-low and simmer for 5 minutes, whisking frequently. If you do not stir the sauce, it will bubble over and burn on your stove—be careful!

3. Remove from the heat and let the sauce cool completely before transferring to a jar. Leftovers will keep in the fridge for up to 10 days.

date-sweetened teriyaki sauce

Let's be honest: Teriyaki sauce is downright delicious. What's not so great, though, is the heaps of sugar and preservatives that often sneak their way into store-bought sauces. The good news is that making your own at home is incredibly fast and easy—and gives you total control over the ingredients! This recipe is moderately spicy and sweet, but not too sweet—if you want to increase or decrease either, simply add or reduce the levels of ginger, garlic, and/or sweetener. Speaking of sweetener, I opt to use Medjool dates here to keep things refined sugar–free. They provide a deeper, more complex flavor than table sugar, plus their natural fibers help to give the sauce more body.

The arrowroot powder helps to make this sauce thick and glossy, which is important if you're using the sauce for the Golden Cauliflower Wings (page 132) or the Sheet Pan Teriyaki Bowls (page 171). If you're looking for a thinner, marinade-style dipping sauce, you can leave it out.

½ cup (120 ml) low-sodium tamari

4 Medjool dates, pitted

1 to 2 cloves garlic, peeled

1-inch (2.5 cm) knob of fresh ginger, peeled

½ tablespoon arrowroot powder (optional)

1 tablespoon maple syrup or coconut sugar

1. Put the tamari, dates, garlic, ginger, arrowroot powder (if using), and maple syrup in a high-speed blender with ¾ cup (180 ml) water. Blend on high speed until a smooth sauce forms, 30 to 40 seconds.

2. Pour the liquid into a medium saucepan over medium-high heat, whisking frequently. Remove from the heat when bubbles begin to form around the edges of the sauce; whisk the mixture once more to form a uniform sauce, then set aside to cool completely. Store in an airtight container in the fridge for up to 10 days.

chipotle enchilada sauce

I originally created this enchilada sauce to use in Chipotle Jackfruit Enchiladas (page 174), but you can also drizzle it over nachos, burrito bowls, tacos, tofu scramble, or use it wherever you would typically use hot sauce. Most enchilada sauces start by frying the spices in oil, but dry-toasting them in a nonstick saucepan produces a similar effect.

All of the heat from this sauce comes from the chipotle peppers in adobo, so use them sparingly if you are sensitive to spice. The peppers themselves come in a can, often found in the international or Mexican food section of the grocery store. You'll only need a couple for this recipe, but you can transfer the saucy leftovers into a different, sealable container and store them in your fridge for several months.

1   tablespoon ancho chile powder

1   teaspoon ground cumin

½   teaspoon garlic powder

⅛   teaspoon ground cinnamon

2   cups (480 ml) vegetable broth

3   tablespoons tomato paste

2 to 4   chipotle peppers in adobo

2   tablespoons arrowroot powder

½   teaspoon pink Himalayan salt

     Juice of ½ lime

1. Heat a medium nonstick saucepan over medium-high heat, then add the chile powder, cumin, garlic powder, and cinnamon. Dry-toast the spices in the pan until fragrant, 60 to 90 seconds.

2. Transfer the toasted spices to a blender with the broth, tomato paste, chipotle peppers, arrowroot powder, and salt. Blend on high speed for 20 to 30 seconds, until a uniform liquid forms. Pour the liquid back into the saucepan, then bring to a boil over high heat, whisking occasionally.

3. When the mixture starts to bubble, reduce the heat to medium-low and cook for an additional 60 to 90 seconds, until the sauce is thick and glossy. Remove from the heat, then whisk in the lime juice. Let the sauce cool completely before pouring into an airtight container and storing in the fridge, where it will last for up to 1 week.

jalapeño ranch

Ranch was always my favorite dressing growing up. I drowned my salads in it, ate it with pizza, and even used it as a dip for green beans and broccoli. It's pretty dairy-heavy, though; most recipes often call for a combination of milk and sour cream. Oddly enough, the combination of dill pickle brine (aka the juice from a jar of dill pickles) and nutritional yeast seems to give a similar flavor!

This jalapeño ranch has a fun spicy twist, but you can just as easily leave out the jalapeño for a more classic flavor. Hemp hearts add some much-needed creaminess here, all while being a good source of omegas, vitamin E, and protein—2 tablespoons have over 6 grams of protein! This dressing is absolutely perfect when drizzled over some Giant Green Bowls (page 161), but you can also use it as a dip for veggies, pizza crusts, or whatever your heart desires.

---

1 cup (145 g) hemp hearts

1 jalapeño, seeds removed

2 tablespoons dill pickle brine

Juice of 1 small lemon (1 to 2 tablespoons)

½ teaspoon dried parsley

½ teaspoon onion powder

1 teaspoon nutritional yeast

⅛ teaspoon paprika

½ teaspoon pink Himalayan salt, or more to taste

1 tablespoon chopped fresh chives

1 teaspoon chopped fresh dill

1. Put the hemp hearts, jalapeño, pickle brine, lemon juice, parsley, onion powder, nutritional yeast, paprika, and salt in a blender with ½ cup plus 2 tablespoons (150 ml) water. Blend for 30 to 45 seconds on high speed, until smooth and creamy.

2. Season with additional salt, if necessary. Add the chives and dill to the blender and pulse until combined, but slightly chunky. Pour into a sealable glass container and use as desired. Leftovers will keep in the fridge for up to 5 days.

nut-free vegan ricotta

Ricotta cheese is actually pretty simple to veganize—it's mild in flavor, and it's relatively easy to re-create that creamy-but-fluffy texture with the combination of some tofu and plant-based fat. I used to make ricotta using cashews, but found that soaked sunflower seeds work as a wonderful nut-free alternative.

The recipe below is a doctored-up, savory version—perfect for stuffing in some Spaghetti Squash Lasagna Boats (page 184). It's also a great replacement in any savory application that typically uses ricotta cheese: think stuffed shells, baked ziti, or as a spread on toast. Alternatively, you can cut the nutritional yeast in half and omit the garlic and Italian seasoning to create a milder, more "classic" ricotta that can be used in both savory and sweet recipes, such as cannoli, baked goods, or fruity dips. However you make and serve it, it's sure to satisfy!

---

1   (14-ounce/395 g) block extra-firm tofu, drained

1   cup (140 g) sunflower seeds, soaked in water overnight and drained

1   tablespoon nutritional yeast

4   cloves garlic, peeled

Juice of 1 small lemon (1 to 2 tablespoons)

1   teaspoon salt-free Italian seasoning

½   teaspoon pink Himalayan salt

Freshly ground black pepper

1. Put the tofu, sunflower seeds, nutritional yeast, garlic, lemon juice, Italian seasoning, and salt in a food processor. Process for 1 minute, then scrape the sides of the device with a spatula. Process for an additional minute, then season with pepper to taste.

2. Transfer the ricotta to a storage container and store in the fridge for up to 1 week. Use as desired.

note: Forgot to soak your sunflower seeds? Put them in a small pot, cover with water, and bring to a boil, then remove from the heat and let the seeds sit in the hot water until tender, 7 to 10 minutes.

index

acknowledgments

There are so many people I need to thank, I don't even know where to begin! I guess I'll start with my parents—thanks for conceiving me, feeding me, and believing in me—this book (and me) *literally* wouldn't be here without you.

A very special thank-you to my partner Dylan, for tasting all the things, doing most of the dishes, and offering endless support during a very busy, tiring, and stressful time in my life. You've done more than you realize, and I would have needed a *lot* more therapy sessions if it weren't for your awesome hugs. I'd also like to thank our dog, Lily, for the silent kitchen support and free floor cleanups.

Thank you to all of my cookbook-writing friends, especially Jackie Sobon, who helped to guide me through this daunting and totally unfamiliar process. Timmy, Lauren, and Jessica, too—*all* of you are so inspiring to me, and I feel lucky to have you in my life.

Thanks to my real-life friends and family, particularly Meg, Jasmine, and all the PNW Fam. For sharing my excitement with me, and for understanding that I needed to go into hiding for a bit while I cranked this book out. Now, let's go get some drinks and Thai food!

Big thanks go to my literary agent, Janis, and my publisher, Holly. This book is now the best it could possibly be, thanks to your uplifting support and constructive feedback. I'm sorry if any typos snuck through, but hey, we're human.

Thank you to Phyllis and Troy, for hosting me in the most gorgeous cottage in the woods while I finished these final chapters. And to Bex, for keeping Lily occupied while I typed away.

A special shoutout goes to the *From My Bowl* recipe-testing group—you guys know who you are! Thank you for blindly trusting me by committing to try these recipes. Also, thank you for telling me when something wasn't good enough, so I could make it better. And a *big* thanks to Josh, my assistant, for holding down the *'Bowl* and doing all of the back-end work that I sure-as-heck didn't want to do.

Finally, thank *you*! Yes, you. The person holding this book. Your support means the world to me, and at the end of the day, that's why I do what I do. So put this thing down for a second, and give yourself a nice pat on the back. Or a bubble bath—those are pretty great, too.

Editor: Holly Dolce
Designer: Jennifer K. Beal Davis
Production Manager: Larry Pekarek

Library of Congress Control Number: 2020931029

ISBN: 978-1-4197-4757-1

Text copyright © 2020 Caitlin Shoemaker
Photographs copyright © 2020 From My Bowl LLC

Cover © 2020 Abrams

Printed and bound in the United States

10 9 8 7 6 5 4 3 2

Abrams books are available at special discounts when purchased in quantity for premiums and promotions as well as fundraising or educational use. Special editions can also be created to specification. For details, contact specialsales@abramsbooks.com or the address below.

Abrams® is a registered trademark of Harry N. Abrams, Inc.

ABRAMS The Art of Books
195 Broadway, New York, NY 10007
abramsbooks.com